NEW POEMS

1963

THE P.E.N. ANTHOLOGIES
OF CONTEMPORARY POETRY

already published

by

Hutchinson of London

*

NEW POEMS 1960

Edited by Anthony Cronin, Jon Silkin, Terence Tiller
with a Foreword by Alan Pryce-Jones

*

NEW POEMS 1961

Edited by William Plomer, Anthony Thwaite, Hilary Corke
with an Introduction by the Editors

*

NEW POEMS 1962

Edited by Patricia Beer, Ted Hughes, Vernon Scannell
with an Introduction by the Editors

*

The first seven P.E.N. anthologies were published
by Michael Joseph Ltd.
New Poems 1952, 1953, 1954, 1955, 1956, 1957, 1958

NEW POEMS

1963

A P.E.N. Anthology of Contemporary Poetry

Edited by
LAWRENCE DURRELL

HUTCHINSON OF LONDON

HUTCHINSON & CO. (*Publishers*) LTD
178-202 Great Portland Street, London, W.1

London Melbourne Sydney
Auckland Bombay Toronto
Johannesburg New York

First published 1963

This book has been set in Spectrum type face. It has been printed in Great Britain by The Anchor Press, Ltd., in Tiptree, Essex, on Smooth Wove paper.

ACKNOWLEDGEMENTS

Acknowledgements are due to the following publications which have included in their pages the poems indicated:

Ambit for the poems by Barry Bowes.
The Cambridge Review for the poem by John Horder.
The Cornhill for *The Burning Bush* by Richard Church.
The Critical Quarterly for the poem by Edward Lucie-Smith.
Encounter for the poems by Nissim Ezekiel and Stephen Spender, and *Sick Child* by Anthony Thwaite.
Expression for the poem by Carl Bode.
The Glasgow Herald for the poem by Derek Stanford.
Harper's for *Her Husband* by Ted Hughes.
The Jewish Quarterly for the poem by Paul Casimir.
John O' London's for *An Italian Afternoon* by Joan Forman and the poem by John Horder.
The Listener for the poem by Charles Causley, for *End Of A Colony* by D. J. Enright, *The Great Beasts* by G. Rostrevor Hamilton, the poems by Elizabeth Jennings and Richard Kell, *Boredom* by George MacBeth, *Tenuous And Precarious* by Stevie Smith and *Notes For A Myth* by Terence Tiller.
The London Magazine for the poems by Robert Conquest, C. Day Lewis and Roy Fuller, for *A Crab* by Thom Gunn, for the poems by Zofia Ilinska, Elizabeth Jennings, Philip Larkin, Bernard Spencer and for *The Boys* by Anthony Thwaite and *Continuum* by Terence Tiller.
Mermaid Festival Of Poetry for *Tulips* by Sylvia Plath.
The New Statesman And Nation for *Back* by A. Alvarez and the poems by Donald Davie and Ted Hughes.
The New Yorker for the poems by Sylvia Plath.
The Noble Savage for the poem by Oonagh Lahr.
The Observer for *The Goddess* by Thom Gunn, the poems by B. C.

Leale, for *She Ghosts . . .* by Peter Redgrove and the poem by Charles Tomlinson.

Phoenix (Liverpool University magazine) for the poem by Joy Udloff.

Poetry Chicago for *Love Affair* by A. Alvarez and the poems by G. S. Fraser and Michael Hamburger.

Punch for *Fur And Feather* by Richard Church.

Review Of English Literature for the poem by Raymond Wilson.

Selection (published by the boys of Winchester School) for the poem by Clifford Dyment.

The Spectator for the poem by Kingsley Amis.

Technology for *The Swarm* by Peter Redgrove.

Three Arts Quarterly for the poem by Mervyn Peake.

The Times Literary Supplement for the poems by Julian Ennis, Mary Hacker and *Dreaming In The Shanghai Restaurant* by D. J. Enright.

Traffic With Time (Khayat's Beirut) for the poem by Christopher Scaife.

Transatlantic Review for the poem by Karen Gershon.

The Western Daily Press for the poem by Zulfikar Ghose.

X Review for *The Last Turn Of The Screw* by Stevie Smith and the poem by David Wright.

The Yorkshire Post for *Incident In City Street* by W. Price Turner.

Acknowledgements are also due to the Third Programme of the British Broadcasting Corporation for poems by the following which have been broadcast: Clifford Dyment, G. S. Fraser, Zulfikar Ghose, Gordon Gridley (*Turning*), Michael Hamburger, Zofia Ilinska, Elizabeth Jennings, Richard Kell, Peter Redgrove (*The Swarm*), John Heath-Stubbs, Terence Tiller and Raymond Wilson.

CONTENTS

INTRODUCTION

The P.E.N. anthology is, by intention, a log-book of the year's work in poetry but it is doubtful if it will ever fulfil its task to the satisfaction of its editors. Time factors hamper it; poets being the wayward creatures they are all too often publish a splendid poem a week too late or too early for inclusion. Others, among the stars of the first magnitude, find their work already bespoke, or signal a temporarily empty notebook to the despair of an editor anxious to make as inclusive and complete a job as possible. This year, however, a number of good poets who had not contributed spontaneously were kind enough to respond to a personal invitation and send along a few of their recent poems. One is particularly grateful to the generosity of Dame Edith Sitwell who responded by sending in the proofs of her latest book: this was treasure trove to the harassed editor all too conscious that his book was going to suffer from a feeling of incompleteness if it could not secure the participation of at least one of our major poets.

The field of choice for this year's work was a very large one; hundreds of poems flowed in from every corner of the Commonwealth and even from Europe; and the general standard of the work was surprisingly, even exasperatingly, high. I say 'exasperating' because had space permitted I could have added about twenty pages more of poetry to this compilation without prejudicing its quality.

But with all these limitations in mind, and all questions of personal preference set on one side, I think that this P.E.N. anthology does present a coherent pattern from which the reader may get an idea of the present estate of poetry; its current shades of preoccupation with various styles and approaches, as well as the theoretical considerations which are agitating the minds of poets today. I have tried to include examples of the work of those who are trying to carve out severely anti-rhetorical and anti-evocative poems in a style which may seem to some too deliberately strained—a style which one might describe as Phenomenological in its severity. But I have tried to counterspring them with work in other styles, more graphic and less austere. I have presented my poets in roughly alphabetical order.

I hope the reader will not only derive great pleasure from the large number of fine poems in the book but also be able to sense its general pattern and shape; he will also, I believe, find himself forced to concede that while work of this calibre is being done, nobody can claim that English poetry is not flourishing.

LAWRENCE DURRELL

NEW POEMS

1963

Kingsley Amis

THE BIG STORE

A rattle, a woollen ball,
A cuddly animal,
Are guaranteed harmless.
A flameproof nightdress
(5 to 7 years)
Is pretty. Water-colours
And painting-book will
Keep someone out of trouble
And not make much mess.

Across the aisle are tiers
Of stuff we use on others
As soon as we can: men's
Two-tone cardigans;
Earrings; rings; pens.

Alasdair Aston

INTO DAWN

The ambulance will always call again.
That early morning nearly three years gone
The three of us set out on jolting roads—
My futile self, my wife, our unborn son,
Whose coming was uncertain as a cord
On which all life's immensities depend—
Set out on dreadful travel into dawn
Where trolleys waited, all the abstract sense,
The clinical appurtenance to love
In centuries of miracle and birth:
And loving mouths more loving under masks
And rubbered hands more gentle than the skin,
Cubicular, compartmented, made man
Of what had seemed mere hopelessness within.
And if he seemed miraculous, that smile
With words and mighty shoulders of a man
At two years old could drag me back to birth
With superstitious terror, or perhaps
Prediction of this blank paralysis,
As, years come round, I yield him back to hands
More capable than these of loving acts,
Hands that revived a marvel past despair—
As this is now that goes out to their care.

A. Alvarez

LOVE AFFAIR

The sun sees many flowers, but the flower sees only the sun:
Blinded three parts of the day, or dark all dark,
Uneasy, cold, attentive for release,
He crouches through the night, or burns and swells
Blindly as in a kind of hurt of love.
They call it blossoming. The unwieldy earth
Clamps round, his sap distrained and petals shrunk.

And nothing is said. The sun moves on above
Indifferent, raging in its own sweet fire
And light, light, light, the flower twists for it,
Straining its mouth for death, which it calls love.
'A god has come upon me', gapes the flower
As over the lip of the earth the sun sinks down.
The moon swings to and fro between the trees
Its casual, icy face. The first leaves fall.

A. Alvarez

BACK

The night I came back from the hospital, scarcely
Knowing what had happened or when,
I went through the whole performance again in my dreams.
Three times—in a dance, in a chase and in something
Now lost—my body was seized and shaken
Till my jaw swung loose, my eyes were almost out
And my trunk was stunned and stretched with a vibration
Sharper than fear, closer than pain. It was death.
So I sweated under the sheets, afraid to sleep,
Though you breathed all night quietly enough by my side.

Was it the *tremor mortis*, the last dissolution
Known now in dreams, unknown in the pit itself
When I was gripped by the neck till my life shook
Like loosening teeth in my head? Yet I recall
Nothing of death but the puzzled look on your face,
Swimming towards me, weeping, clouded, uncertain,
As they took the tube from my arm
And plugged the strange world back in place.

Dannie Abse

THE NAMELESS

There is the eight hour sleep and the forgetting,
and the leaving behind: the nameless things,
or rather the unnameable—no frosted windowpane,
not even an empty playground after rain.
Yet to reach for the unidentifiable
we list such images; it seems we're unable
to exorcize, or diminish, or claim
what arrives, at desolate moments, home.

And even music is memory that has faded.

Still we categorize: a key turning round a lock,
the odour in a public telephone box,
as going into a great distance the days,
like snowed-over footsteps, sink down the maze
of unremembering: a hole in the eye,
a chasm in the senses below the memory,
and we are called, though our names are not ours
till carved on the gravestone for hours and hours.

Andrew Baily

CHILDREN AND WATER

As children we would go to a spring
And move a stone from its mouth to watch
Water come, and wrinkle out into the sun,
Silver as Christmas paper over the stone beds,
And through the green-turned paper of the leaves.
As poets, we would remove the stone from the mouth,
So the water runs smooth, and crisp, and finished.

Jack Beeching

NEVER BUT NOW—XVI

Across the bar our gilded dead men shine,
Their blood it was disguised this dust in wine.

Out from the hillside juts a drystone wall
To mark the edge where fields and builders fall.

There as the vineyard into woodland turns
A charcoal-burner burning charcoal burns.

And so we bleed, fall, burn; so burn, build, drink.
Some think on death, some die before they think.

Barry Bowes

WHO IN THE LEAVES

who in the leaves
blown at an autumn wall
whose sound in the cobbled entry
behind me

what the light through curtains
like a long scottie dog,
who stands at the foot of my bed
dark and eyeless and

i hear the kettle whistle a name
a cry in the street my attention
running my following
to speak long time no see
a cough my commander a laugh
my executioner

who in the tree watching me over
whose hand at my shoulder
makes my panic
what scampers along the shore
a dog pawing the wall jumping falling
on fours and sadly keeping pace
never to reach me

what looks of frightened scrutiny
to die and let the eyes fall
and in the night each figure
to be eliminated

someone follows me through grass

i expect to turn in the crowd
and find a kind of jesus.

Carl Bode

THE NOCTURNE

Why the hell do you use all that black
In your painting, my neighbour asks across the fence.
I thumb my canvasses, the oboes going slack,
Flutes elegantly wailing, the colours colours of elegance.

Of course the concert stops; the composer done,
He wipes his hand upon a greasy rag of fire
Replying flatly that he was only having fun
And who the hell are you, may I inquire?

You crane your neck upon the latest night.
It shapes and opens up into arcades
And avenues and pergolas of light.
Your eye, now leading its battalions on invades
The widening valleys, the martial music bright
With scimitars; and everywhere the neighbours lean on spades.

Charles Causley

DEVONPORT

I saw two sailors in Devonport city,
Their bones were of shell and their eyes were marine.
Never forget, said the one to the other,
The deeds we have done and the sights we have seen.

As they came down Ker Street by Devonport Column,
By the Egyptian and Oddfellows' Hall,
No sound was heard from the Nile-voiced oracle,
Beak-faced, indifferent, marching the wall.

In the Old Chapel I sat with my doxy,
Down came the sun with its streamers of gin,
Down by the Forum a blind-fingered fiddler
Felt for a tune that was crazy as sin.

Empty the gallows-rope blew on the morning,
Empty your heart when you wake up in bed,
Stare in despair at the face there beside you,
Find that, like you, it is dead, it is dead.

I went down Fore Street, the summer descending,
Turning my voice on the rim of the tide,
Do you recall how we three sailed together?
We never heard of you, mister, they cried.

Swore that whenever misfortune befell us
Nothing should sever the word I now speak?
Only the wind shoving down from the Dockyard
Troubled the waters about Stonehouse Creek.

Lightly they walked on the lap of the morning,
Their hair was of pitch and their tongues sweet as tar,
While high in the heaven a love-killed old kitehawk
Bawled on the blue like an opera star.

Blithely O blithely the casual morning
Burned life away as the leaf on a tree,
Only the sun spun its mad hoop beside me
And down at the end of the street crowed the sea.

Paul Casimir

JEWISH RISING: WARSAW 1943

A woman hides a child,
A skirt blows in the wind,
And pressed like five candles,
Fingers burn their shapes on a wall.
But we can be none of these things.

To be dumb is to be afraid
Not of lost dignity, ourselves petty,
(For our dignity lessened
Adds nothing to their death)
But we can be none of these things.

The wind took their ashes,
The river their indelible footsteps,
The grey sky their white, cold smiles.
Somewhere a stone is black with five fingers.
But we can be none of these things.

Richard Church

FUR AND FEATHER

He can't touch feathers. He can touch fur.
An old man now, but all his life
He's been that way. He fell in love.
The young woman made no demur,
And married him. He and his wife
Raised a family, since gone
To the world's ends. Then he lost her,
And now he mostly lives alone
Writing to where his children rove
When he gets an address. But still
He cleans his pipe with a woollen thread
And dare not use a chicken-quill
To oil the grandfather clock. Absurd,
This lifelong something, this blood-taboo
That will not let him handle a bird.
But watch him go out to the garden loo
You'll see the robins follow him there.
Further afield, by moor and hill
Where he likes to wander, no lapwing will bother
To droop a wing, to make him leave
His chosen path and take another.
But should he stoop to stroke a cat
It will spark with hate and disappear.
Dogs dislike the shape of his hat,
Or the way he walks. He tries in vain
To coax a squirrel or mouse to hand,
And cows move off as he draws near.
It's a matter hard to understand.
No philosopher knows whether
He, or beasts, or birds in their fear
Are wrong, or why he can't withstand
Desire for fur, while dreading feather.

Richard Church

THE BURNING BUSH

Repeating the Beatitudes
Instead of prayer,
I knelt before the Burning Bush
But found none there
To condone or echo my voice.
The deep universal hush
Of God-covering solitudes
Mantled every noise;
The padded paw, the bird
Fanning air with downy wings,
And earth's quite silent things,
The rocks, mosses, ferns,
Substance never heard
In the orchestra of decay.

The Bush, that buds even as it burns
In dreadful equilibrium,
Let its fiery branches sway
Over the Kingdom that shall come
Lit by timeless Day.

Then the voice, so still, so small,
Budded as a flame,
Blossomed in soliloquy,
But still it named no name.
Light shivered, the flame began to fall,
And stars to prick the sky.
'*I am*', and then again, '*I am*',
Was heard by all mankind in me.
It was a sound for eyes to see,
A flower for ears to hear,
A perfume for the tongue.
It had a grace that leaned forlorn

Above a creature newly born,
With music mortally sung,
'*I am*—but also death shall be
The blessing that you crave,
The blessing after life is done,
The glory in the grave.
I am—re-risen in my Son.'

Robert Conquest

SEAL ROCKS: SAN FRANCISCO

Quite close to the abrupt city
Set on a circuit of bay,
Rocks shrug off the Pacific
A cable-length from the cliff:
Non-humans inhabit that spray.

Last night in a North Beach bar
I was shown, by a fine poet,
Arrangements of syllables
To the levity of dance
And the labour of thought.

Which it's tempting to match with
The accomplished arc, all
The swing of the seal's dive,
His romping swim in
A sun-and-spray sparkle.

How can a real being
Float, tamed to another's
Symbol, though? The differences,
Escaping such aquaria,
Plunge superb. Yet reminders,

Connectives merely, may
Splash illumination
Over his hot solids:
If his tight fury is absent
May spin the wake of his action

Across the more often forgotten:
Arrogance of pure art,
And gross humour of enjoyment.
—The blue heave bans all set
Choreographies, for a start:

Not trying to be, just being,
Subduing the willed; the poem
Living the poet; all that move
Amphibious, so emerging
Out of a dark, deep medium

Where they can live but not breathe.
Meanwhile, watching these
Big-eyed, unanxious sea-things,
We can enjoy the merely
Actual: a good thing for verse.

Hilary Corke

A MAN'S SONG

In deeper fat the sense of sin retires;
The inhibitions and their prohibitions
Are unheard cries in fleshy stillness sunk.
Even in my ashes die my wonted fires:
Age is a kind of getting drunk,
If we believe the Porter,
Removing the performances of provoked desires.
My lust grows longer and my lunger shorter.

Not in this case my secretary but
The daughter of a colleague on the loose
(These changing patterns) she comes each Friday after
Some lunch together to this secret mews
Where I remove her clothing. To some laughter
I do this, we being kind together,
And then begin.
Her hair from her black bun (I pull the pin)
Explodes like a love-grenade, my wounded heifer
Lows in my arms. I have not much to offer
But eke it out with tricks that she pretends
To find too marvellous; but when my hands
Are lifted, my latch is lifted, she will like any
Arrow I know to the bed of a boy friend
Go zinging, to get the straight stuff straight, and all
My lore go lightly down to stallion sweat
And the untutored rage I must forget.

She goes and the lame gate hobbles on its crutch.
She is drowned in taxis and in the aspiring voices
Of urchins; the town machine rolls into night
And the spill of dusk seeps into the un-she'ed room
Lapping about me, who will not go home
But hark to the poor mice in my wall

Whose feet scutter my manhood. The tall
Pierglass (mirror of love) looms, my waist
Thickens, the dark curls climb.
I burn and will not sleep, it is not yet time.

All in the evil nadir the merchants' bells
And chiming of the city pinnacles
Mark out the board of death. One by one
My driven pawn steps over, white and wan
To what black queen-row? Dawn comes full
Of nothing as in the window's square
The whole sour night unwinds its sullen wool.
She sleeps where, asprawl like a smashed star?
Far, far in a boy's angle, lost and far.

Then O you serene jealousy, must I learn,
Unmarried cuckold, to smiling take your taunt,
To cage no birds, to grin
Like pyknic nuncle as the kris goes in,
Nor grudge her anywhere nor all her cries
In alien air, but she will still be ranging
Nor I pursue but in an easy chair
Sit crucified to watch her colours changing?

Bee in the shrivelled rind of forenight's apple
What do I do not in my own tight house
Haunting this Saturday silence, this tumbled linen
Long cold, blurred text
With only a lipstick's footnote? Dust
Has fallen all night on the dove-pocked sill I lean on,
And in a midnight vexed
By long longing the clock stopped. I do ill
Jumping the gun with a ghost. I burn of will.

The spent flower dries in the meadow,
The young flower in the pollened air
Is covered by any weather
In the community of bird-cries, the unowned

Rustle of papery leaf and everyone's rain.
My dark whiles boom in my head, I will buy her
This garnet heart against her coming,
To bear wherever she is homing
Although it be not here
Nor ever again next year.

I burn.
Return, return;
Me by my own emptiness consumed,
O flesh not mine nor the years', revive, resume!

Donald Davie

A CHRISTENING

What we do best is breed:
August Bank Holiday, whole
Populations explode

Across the wolds and in a slot
Of small cars pullulate
By couples. Millington meadows

Flower with campstools. At
Beverley the font
Has a cover carved like a goblet.

The new baby is fed.
I stumble back to bed.
I hear the owls for a long time

Hunting. Or are they never
In the winter grey of before dawn,
Those pure long quavers,

Cries of love? I put my arms around you.
Small mice freeze among tussocks.
The baby wails in the next room.

Upstairs Mrs Ramsay
Dies, and the house
Is full of the cries of the new-born.

In red and smoky wood
A follower of Wren
Carved it at Beverley:

The generous womb that drops
Into the sanctified water immediate fruit.
What we do best is breed.

Martin Daniel

SOLITARY ORDER

Retreat
succeeds defeat
as she composing
her tracery of shells
                                        of thoughts exploding light
into a rigid order, capital
of solitude
                                        disowns, stifles her own children
adopts the forms of stone
                                        statutes of silence
drapery statues
                                        settles for expectation.

Then she of pains fears
drawn lines decisions
deaths (except death) desires

But also of bathing in sun
of birds' flight
shouting of children
Or
communication with any stranger's smile
What of these does she have?

Nun.

C. Day Lewis

THE ROOM

(for George Seferis)

To this room—it was somewhere at the palace's
Heart, but no one, not even visiting royalty
Or reigning mistress, ever had been inside it—
To this room he'd retire.
Graciously giving himself to, guarding himself from
Courtier, suppliant, stiff ambassador,
Supple assassin, into this unviewed room
He, with the air of one urgently called from
High affairs to some yet loftier duty,
Dismissing them all, withdrew.

And we imagined it suitably fitted out
For communing with a God, for meditation
On the Just City; or, at the least, a bower of
Superior orgies. . . . He
Alone could know the room as windowless
Though airy, bare yet filled with the junk you find
In any child-loved attic; and how he went there
Simply to taste himself, to be reassured
That under the royal action and abstraction
He lived in, he was real.

Clifford Dyment

THE RAVEN

A raven crouched in a tree.
It lived in the sky like me.

I stared at the night in the tree:
I felt its eye warm me.

What shock was shaking the tree?
Why was there blood on me?

From the world into the tree
Stones sprang and hissed round me.

They were killing the bird in the tree,
The raven that cheered me.

I hurried out of my tree—
The people greeted me:

They saw no bird in the tree.
They were very friendly to me.

D. J. Enright

END OF A COLONY

The groups break up;
As if they'd thought of other loyalties.
The characters count their compensation,
And leave for some Aegean island.
No one replaces them;
The groups break up.

These in their heyday
Were centres of articulate light:
Bright sparks who fought the dying fire,
Found their own people not their sort;
Lived well on foreign allowances,
And harboured native refugees.

But now the country's free.
And they are not. The government,
They say, is fascist, or communist, or . . .
And any day may see them refugees.
Will those they used to harbour
Harbour them? Loyalties have changed.

The place, they say, is ruled by crooks.
(Wasn't that always so?
Yet so much harder when the crooks
Are not those red-faced ageing men,
When the crooks are your own age,
Or younger, your own pupils even.)

Not everyone's a ruler, though.
Orioles still flash in the trees,
Girls' frocks glow slowly through the dusk,
Talk continues in the cafés.
And the excessive—they still think twice.
What will you do on your Aegean island?

D. J. Enright

DREAMING IN THE SHANGHAI RESTAURANT

I would like to be that elderly Chinese gentleman.
He wears a gold watch with a gold bracelet,
But a shirt without sleeves or tie.
He has good-luck moles on his face, but is not
  disfigured with fortune.
His wife resembles him, but is still a handsome woman,
She has never bound her feet or her belly.
Some of the party are his children, it seems,
And some his grandchildren;
No generation appears to intimidate another.
He is interested in people, without wanting to
  convert them or pervert them.
He eats with gusto, but not with lust;
And he drinks, but is not drunk.
He is content with his age, which has always suited
  him.
When he discusses a dish with the pretty waitress,
It is the dish he discusses, not the waitress.
The tablecloth is not so clean as to show indifference,
Not so dirty as to signify a lack of manners.
He proposes to pay the bill but knows he will not be
  allowed to.
He walks to the door, like a man who doesn't fret
  about being respected, since he is;
A daughter or grand-daughter opens the door for him,
And he thanks her.
It has been a satisfying evening. Tomorrow
Will be a satisfying morning. In between
  he will sleep satisfactorily.
I guess that for him it is peace in his time.
It would be agreeable to be this Chinese gentleman.

Julian Ennis

COLD STORAGE

Headless and hard as bricks, painted off-white,
Hanging like frozen clothes, the dead herd moves
Along the assembly line to the street
Where, in the sawdust, butchers wait with knives.

Here is no slightest hint of buttercups
And daisies, bellowing and having calves,
And Lightfoot coming to the milking shed.
Impossible also to think that shapes
Like these can grace the bodies of our loves
With soft skin and hair and glossy maidenhood.

Unlucky, then, for sacred three-in-one
We cannot correlate existences—
The rank-fat creature, the steak underdone
And oozing blood, and these clean carcasses.

Nissim Ezekiel

PHILOSOPHY

There is a place to which I often go,
Not by planning to, but by a flow
Away from all existence, to a cold
Lucidity, whose will is uncontrolled.
Here, the mills of God are hardly slow.

The landscape in its geologic prime
Dissolves to show its quintessential slime.
A million stars are blotted out. I think
Of each historic passion as a blink
That happened to the sad eye of Time.

But residues of meaning still remain,
As darkest myths meander through the pain
Towards a final formula of light.
I, too, reject that clarity of sight:
What cannot be explained, do not explain.

The mundane language of the senses sings
Its own interpretations. Common things
Become, by virtue of their commonness,
An argument against the nakedness
That dies of cold to find what truth it brings.

John Fairfax

SEA OF TARSHISH

Where the cliff's down defies the sea that wails
And seamen bury long feathers on a wave,
Tarshish calls her mastership that sails
Loosely seawards—a thin brown hand would save
Your guess. Stop and listen. For an ark
Is part boat, part charity. Wrecked on coral
These mariners are tongue-tied as seals bark
To windward and bite on rocks of oracle.

There is no waste, no drifting in a city,
Anchor you sea; be still, O ships and wings.
All that crawls upon this land is crucified.
See these foiling waters, there our city:
There on the cliffs we hoist cradles and kings
So what is true in fantasy must ride.

Joan Forman

AN ITALIAN AFTERNOON

The dusty veil of silence, light as silk,
Lies on the hanging bell of the afternoon.
The cicada and cypress rustle
Add small music to the mode of meditation.
Crude as granite, the hammered slopes
Rear and cavort above the village;
The earth horse climbs
Into the bowl of sky.

But where the marbled steps descend
And naiad-plunge within the lake,
Reposes peace, white dragonfly,
Forever winged and ever whole;
Phoenician, Roman, squatting boy,
Stretch hands to take, lean reckless over
The malachite gloom.

The wings depend on silence;
All the glass and sapphires of this world will close
With the sweet tone of the angelus
And the high notes of house-laughter.

Joan Forman

THE TENDRIL ARIADNE HELD

The thought sprung fine as floss
From a forsaken hedgerow—
Spider-twined round briony and thorn
Leading on to ploughed lands
And the clean airs of the mind.

Memory haunts the woodland.
Child in stream and tree
Calls to its cloudy fellows.
Maiden gleans the cornfield,
Building from scattered seed
A brazen shield to keep her.

Swift Pan-faces peer
Mocking the empty woodland ways
Where once the old gods walked,
And now their empty towers
Reel to the wind and the cry
Of owls and the mating foxes.

There are lost things in the wood;
Old dreams, old gods, old loves,
Where the hearts beat through the elms
With a green, uncaring passion.

It was fashioned so in the old time,
And now the thread gives colour to it all—
The tendril Ariadne held
To lead her lover home.

Edgar Foxall

TWO POEMS
FROM
THE ISLES OF BUCOLIA

I

The cock crew unnaturally
for it was early evening
when I was subject to a vision
of five balding guests
risen from drunken sleep

loud
        loud were the curses
of their five strumpets

outside with the brightness
of old horse brasses
the evening burned and smiled
it was Christ knows beautiful

but what was the meaning
of the boozed balding guests
the five cursing strumpets
struggling with rubber corsets

was it that satisfaction
of dog-day desires
certainly brings no great
amount of evening peace

apart from that
                        don't ask me
I've had little education.

II

Where falls that brief hand now
that once on grape and wine glasses
fell like a sigh

she   though I don't indulge
in these light memories too frequently
occurred to me

from out an incident as trite
and commonplace as a thin lip
seen in the glow

of neon milklight at the point
where two roads cross and traffic halts
and there it was

the memory upon the mist
the insubstantial hand that she
pressed on the glass

a strangeness   yet I lack the art
to fix the range of it entire
the chill   the lure

Tennyson would have found the word
alive and common to the task
usual   yet pure.

G. S. Fraser

CATULLUS: XXII

Varus, you know Suffenus well. He is
handsome, and quite a wit, and nicely mannered,
and the most copious scribbler in the world.
He must have written quite ten thousand verses
or more, and not like other folk on scraps
but on imperial paper, in new rolls,
new bosses, fine red ribbon, parchment covers,
all with ruled lines, and all smoothed out with pumice;
and when you read these this smooth pretty fellow
suddenly seems a goat-herd or a navvy—
it's so absurd, and such a total change!
What shall we say about this? Here's a man
more than just bright and gay and affable
who suddenly becomes a hick of hicks,
taking up poetry; yet a man who's never
really so happy as when writing poems—
that's what he likes and worships in himself!
Well, we all fall this way! There's not a person
whom in some matter you can fail to see
to be Suffenus. We cart round our follies,
but cannot see the bags upon our backs.

G. S. Fraser

OVID: AMORES, I, 5

Sultry it was, and the day had passed its noontide:
    I stretched myself on the middle of my bed.
One shutter of the window open, I had closed the other:
    What light came through was such as you find in woods
Or a glow like dusk's with the sun just disappearing,
    Or light night just gone, and daylight not yet here.
It was such a light as would suit a backward maiden
    Whose shy shame hopes to find some covering—
And, in fact, Corinna came, in a girdled tunic,
    And her fair hair flowing on each side of her neck,
The very spit of the way the great Semiramis
    Went to her bed, and much-embracèd Lais.
I tore her gown off—not that it veiled her greatly;
    But she struggled a bit to be covered by it still,
Yet, even as she fought, not wholly hoping to conquer;
    I won the fight, since she did not wish to win.
She stood before me with her thin gown fallen:
    In all her body I could find no stain.
What shoulders I saw (and touched them, too), what arms,
    And her paps' roundness—how ripe they were to be
                                                                pressed!
What a level plain, under her breast, her belly;
    What grand, great flanks; and what a youthful thigh!
Need I catalogue details? I saw nothing unlovely,
    And her naked body I crushed to my naked own.
Write the rest for yourselves!

                                    Tired, at last, we slept quietly.
May such a noontide often come my way!

Roy Fuller

BAGATELLES

Too self-indulgent, poetry.
Stepping outside this morning, a drop
Fell from the gutter on my pen,
Subsequently diluting these words.
Or who could want to hear about
My boring love, myopic eye
That blurs the world of kings, examines
A portly spider tickling its navel
With the arms of a Hindu deity.

Geranium petals, fingernails
Of little oriental whores,
Scattered on summer stone.

This mole beneath her hair in the nape
Might be a deformity were she not
Lovely: is a deformity.

I stop my car to let a girl,
Carrying a dog, cross the road;
And think 'Girl with a Dog', but wonder
If in fact art is better than life.

Stain the stuff lightly with umber,
The eyes and foliage wash in
With running brown, and scumble breasts,
Thighs, belly, with a famished brush.
Closeness to life depends on the scumbled hand,
Distance from art upon the running eye.

Early morning: my cat at first refuses food,
Wishing to be reassured, no doubt, after the night.

Distinguishing in the glasses birds
From autumn leaves by an occasional shrug
Instead of the waving and revolving,
A greater glossiness of speckle
Even in the continuous rain,
I know I unfairly evaluate
The world's life, placing first myself,
Whose curiosity and love
Discover how birds make out in winds
That strip the boughs and shake my house.

> Does a big nose go with playing Bach?
> No more than a collection of Van Gogh
> Postcards with the breasts of fourteen.

The chromaticism of '04
That almost anachronistically
We heard encased in whalebone on small
Gilt chairs in rows in gas-lit rooms,

Became the unrelieved agony
Of composers idly shot by soldiers
While taking the air at the end of wars,

Then cascades of notes in the right hand
Against old tunes composed for money,
Improvised beside the sea by negroes
To woo little ears nestling in poignant hair-dos.

> I saw a lady in a car
> Stop the machine and sound two pips
> At which a little milkman quit
> His meaner vehicle and, leaning
> Where she had thoughtfully let down
> The window, kissed her lips.

I walked on jealous of that swain,
Touched none the less by the resource
With which he'd left his sturdy heart
With bottles at her exalted door,
Making their passion mythical
Simply by being coarse.

Karen Gershon

I WAS NOT THERE

The morning they set out from home
I was not there to comfort them
the dawn was innocent with snow
in mockery—it is not true
the dawn was neutral was immune
their shadows threaded it too soon
they were relieved that it had come
I was not there to comfort them

One told me that my father spent
a day in prison long ago
he did not tell me that he went
what difference does it make now
when he set out when he came home
I was not there to comfort him
and now I have no means to know
of what I was kept ignorant

Both my parents died in camps
I was not there to comfort them
I was not there they were alone
my mind refuses to conceive
the life the death they must have known
I must atone because I live
I could not have saved them from death
the ground is neutral underneath

Every child must leave its home
time gathers life impartially
I could have spared them nothing since
I was too young—it is not true
they might have lived to succour me
and none shall say in my defence
had I been there to comfort them
it would have made no difference

Zulfikar Ghose

IN CALCUTTA

A woman, her grey hair swinging in knots
round her shoulders, her sari loose as a drape,
jumps obscenely at a street corner.
Her voice has lost its hysterical note.
No mannerism of face as she leaps,
shakes her hand at her groin, screams the inner

hunger out. Just a beggar-woman, dancing.
Come from what brothel of the imagination
to seduce a few coins of public disgust?
People circumnavigate her, wincing,
as she laughs out the cruellest perversions,
dropping her sari down to her waist.

Should she slip into the river or jump
from Howrah Bridge, no pity would be evoked,
but her pregnant gait and parody of childbirth
hurt the mind. I turn away like a pimp
to count my cash in private. I feel sick.
Why do I hoard the virtues of this earth?

Gordon Gridley

TURNING

Now, after school, hearing the ball
thud on the boarded workshop wall,
I light a cigarette to burn
one more day's rubbish heap of small
vexations. In grateful solitude I turn
from teaching those who have no wish to learn.

A heavy block of red padouk,
fine grained as veined Siena rock,
no less obdurate, hard of heart
as a centre-half at nine o'clock,
lies on the bench. I take a plane and start
to face it; this I have found the hardest part.

On the lathe-head's tight, centrifugal flight
it spins; at the gouge's first raw bite
the whirling wood screams from the wound.
Tricking my intermittent sight,
the rough-hewn block appears already round:
my judgement often fails upon false ground.

Though I cut with steel, I yet can feel
for the rosewood bowl upon the wheel
a kind of love. I have taken care,
for scars in wood can never heal;
in clumsy hands the turner's tools may tear.
I know the responsibility I bear.

Gordon Gridley

A FAMILY MAN

Checked at the traffic lights,
the sidecar driver eyes the solo covertly;
impassive goggles mask the enmity of age
for youth, the hardly self-acknowledged jealousy
of one who has succeeded to his rights.

No interest now, a thing to use,
the aging sidevalve exhausts with nagging monotony;
the solo revs to insolent cacophony;
his rival's empty pillion points the irony
that, choosing, we renounce the right to choose.

Though only thirty-five,
he is much older than one generation;
there is infinity of separation
between the solo and the combination:
an added weight ensures he stays alive.

Easing her through the gears,
reluctant to pass forty, vicariously he heels
the solo round the curve ahead, and honesty,
compelling just respect for skill and symmetry,
reconciles him to his rival and his years.

Thom Gunn

A CRAB

A crab labours across my thigh.
Oh. The first time I got crabs, I

experienced positively
Swiftian self-revulsion: me

unclean! But now I think instead
'I must get some A200,'

and feel (picking it up, watching
its tiny beige legs, a live thing

that wriggles in all directions)
neither disgust nor indifference,

but a fondness, as for a pet.
I'm glad it's nothing worse, and yet

it slipped and swung from one of us
to the other, unfelt because

the skin was alive with so much
else. It was a part of our touch.

Thom Gunn

THE GODDESS

When eyeless fish meet her on
her way upward, they gently
turn together in the dark
brooks. But naked and searching
as a wind, she will allow
no hindrance, none, and bursts up

through potholes and narrow flues
seeking an outlet. Unslowed
by fire, rock, water or clay,
she after a time reaches
the soft abundant soil, which
still does not dissipate her

force—for look! sinewy thyme
reeking in the sunlight; rats
breeding, breeding, in their nests;
and the soldier by a park
bench with his greatcoat collar
up, waiting all evening for

a woman, any woman
whose dress is tight across her
ass as bark in moonlight.
Proserpina! It is we,
vulnerable, quivering,
who stay you to abundance.

G. Rostrevor Hamilton

THE GREAT BEASTS

We have hunted you but given you your greatness:
Planted a foot on you, on tawny pelt,
Sinews limp, the blazing eyes gone dark:
Yet given you greatness:

In the dark mind
Have hunted you with lethal shafts of light
Driven you from your lairs
Prisoned you with the unicorn whitening through
The dusk of tapestries: have made you serve
Our pride in heraldry, yet you in chief
Take the heraldic honour.

For we with fiery words, garnish of paint,
Have persecuted, have exalted you:
And at the beastly greatness we have made
Tremble, as we tremble at four superhuman
Planet-eyed worshipping beasts and the beast
Blasphemous in the Book of Revelation.

G. Rostrevor Hamilton

CONTRITION

Many took his part
    And spoke of things done well.
But he, knowing his heart,
    What tale had he to tell?

Head sunk on his breast;
    Hands that told the same
With ten fingers pressed
    Against a face of flame.

Mary Hacker

ACHTUNG! ACHTUNG!

I'm War. Remember me?
'Yes, you're asleep,' you say, 'and you kill men.'
Look in my game-bag, fuller than you think.

I kill marriages.
If one dies, one weeps and then heals clean.
(No scar without infection.) That's no good.
I can do better when I really try.
I wear down the good small faiths, enough
For little strains of peace, the near, the known,
But not for the big absence, man-sized silences,
Family pack of dangers, primate lusts
I hang on them.

I kill families.
Cut off the roots, the plant will root no more.
Tossed from thin kindness to thin kindness on
The child grows no more love; will only seek
A pinchbeck eros and a tawdry shock.
I teach the race to dread its unborn freak.
I maim well.

I drink gold.
How kind of you to pour it without stint
Into my sleeping throat. In case I die?
You think I'm god, the one that pours the most
Getting my sanction? Well, perhaps you're right.
Divert it, anyway, from use of peace;
Keep the gross gaol, starvation and the lout,
The succulent tumour, loving bacillus, the clot
As bright as mine, friends all. I pop their prey
Into my bag.

I am the game that nobody can win.
What's yours is mine, what's mine is still my own.
I'm War. Remember me.

Norman Harvey

TESTAMENT

The face came in my house and shut the door,
flat as a card with slit-thin eyes and lips
like lines. I could not wine it, being poor
but gave it blood in spoonfuls, sip by sip
and that was all.

I could not kiss that face, so cold, nor talk
to it, no words you see; it could not share
my passionate fire nor without limbs walk
in the ways I trod. It was just flatly there
and that was all.

It drove me mad, so silently around
so obviously feeding on my breath.
I cut it up twelve pieces in the ground
thinking that steel could slice it into death
that would be all.

It could not breed of course, being alone
and incomplete at that, no heart no seed
yet grew twelve equal faces from the one
each with expression flat as thoughtless creed
and that was all.

No chance to shut them out, I lit the fire
put out the usual notes, undid my tie
then hooked my neck inside a ring of wire.
The faces sat a circle round my sigh
and that was all.

Michael Hamburger

THE BODY

Blue sky. White sand the wavelets lick and leave.
Alone his body struts, alone lies down.
Spiced with what springs, tautened in what tart winters
It crouched and ran and leapt and climbed and hung,
Pulled at the oar, to exquisite horsebacks clung,
Rippled and swelled and sweated, flew on skis,
Braved currents, breakers, basked on how many shores.
The fruits and wines of every region fed it,
Beasts, wildfowl, fishes and more curious fauna
Its narrow bulk displaced. To the best winds it went,
Now noon, now morning sun for blending of its colour,
Now high, now low for cordials of air.

None stalks it now to win or to admire,
Nor yet to kill. Of its own prime it dies
Where still he waits for her who in one glance will gather
Those foods, exertions, weathers, distances,
In his true landscape recognizes her lover,
Each dear perfection answered in her eye.
Night took them all; smothers indifferently
Flesh of whatever tint, complexion, shape,
Abetting not the goddess but the woman,
Carnivorous mind more lithe than ever body was
In turning alien substances to gain;
Love, the sole acrobat, all limb and maw.

The sun's eye dims. No eye but his looks there.
A blotted contour, cold, his body struts
On greyish sand the wavelets lick and leave.

John Horder

THE MINDFUL

It is that territory
Where the mindful fear to tread,
Scouring their way for rational posts
Trees to grasp or gates to lean on,
Suspecting my inclination
As I cycle down Sidgwick Avenue at night
Of turning the leaves of the plane trees
Into pieces of paper sculpture,
Tresses of gold supported by wire.

The mindful shiver and hover
Casting care against sadness,
Afraid of the Romantic nightmare
They pause on the word, grasping its meaning
Syntactically yet hardly with feeling.
The point between mind and feeling
Has yet to be found.
One must go beyond the word.

Ted Hughes

HER HUSBAND

Comes home dull with coal-dust deliberately
To grime the sink and foul towels and let her
Learn with scrubbing-brush and scrubbing-board
The stubborn character of money.

And let her learn through what kind of dust
He has earned his thirst and the right to quench it
And what sweat he has exchanged for his money
And the blood-count of money. He'll humble her

With new light on her obligations.
The fried woody chips kept warm two hours in the oven
Are only part of her answer.
Hearing the rest, he claps them to the fire back

And is away round the house-end singing
'Come back to Sorrento' in a voice
Of resounding corrugated iron.
Her back has bunched into a hump as an insult. . . .

For they will have their rights.
Their jurors are to be assembled.
From the little crumbs of soot. Their brief
Goes straight up to heaven and nothing more is heard of it.

Ted Hughes

WODWO

What am I? nosing here, turning leaves over
following a faint stain on the air to the river's edge
I enter water. What am I to split
the glassy grain of water looking upward I see the bed
of the river above me upside down very clear
what am I doing here in mid-air? Why do I find
this frog so interesting as I inspect its most secret
interior and make it my own? Do these weeds
know me and name me to each other have they
seen me before, do I fit in their world? I seem
separate from the ground and not rooted but dropped
out of nothing casually I've no threads
fastening me to anything I can go anywhere
I seem to have been given the freedom
of this place what am I then? And picking
bits of bark off this rotten stump gives me
no pleasure and it's no use so why do I do it
me and doing that have coincided very queerly
But what shall I be called am I the first
have I an owner what shape am I what
shape am I am I huge if I go
to the end on this way past these trees and past these trees
till I get tired that's touching one wall of me
for the moment if I sit still how everything
stops to watch me I suppose I am the exact centre
but there's all this what is it roots
roots roots roots and here's the water
again very queer but I'll go on looking

Zofia Ilinska

THE REFUGEE

You came here twenty years ago, a refugee.
You now possess a British passport; qualify
    for the old-age pension.
Your mother is buried in Ireland.
Your husband is buried in Poland, known as
    Russia in recent maps.
Your brother has finally settled in Montreal.
Your sons went to Malaya to fight bandits;
    went to Africa; went to Canada.
Your daughter breeds pigs in Cornwall writing
    verse in a foreign tongue.
Their letters tell you of crocodiles and apes;
    of great elephants perfectly still
Guarding their tusks in wild places;
    of deep winters and huskies and the
Song of the huskies pitched in a minor key.
Of kingfishers and seagulls and the tides of the
    surrounding sea—until you almost forget
The streams of your childhood.

You understand the language of your in-laws. Of yours
    they have now mastered 'tak i nie'.
Your grandchildren (and one is a cripple) do not speak
    your mother-tongue, but they have learnt
    to call you 'Babcia' which means 'grandmother'.
This is one of your happiest words.
Sometimes you are amused to have such a mongrel family.
Sometimes you think 'this is very strange'.
Sometimes you get muddled which language applies to which.
Sometimes you still take to church your native Missal;
    but seldom now—and only by mistake.
You have said that you dream in English.

* * *

Until the age of forty you have never
    entertained a divorced person in your house.
Until the age of forty you had not known the word
    'homosexual'—yet you were civilized and
    broadminded and not unduly sheltered.

Until the age of forty you had never been short of money;
    then a friend said 'beggars are not choosers'.
You have never missed church on a Sunday.
You have never been to a psychiatrist
You have never said or thought 'I could not care less'.
You have never allowed your suffering to become a
    mental obsession.
You have considered sin to be the greatest evil.

You are now an old woman of great beauty,
    strong and serene,
At home with the elements, and as it were
    used to taming foreigners, birds and squirrels,
And although—unawares—your face drifts off into
    layers of sadness,
This has only been known to happen when gates
    are closed after children,
Or when—in between courses,—a door bangs
    in the draught, and all of a sudden
There is nothing whatsoever to say.

Elizabeth Jennings

SEQUENCE IN HOSPITAL

I. PAIN

At my wits' end
And all resources gone, I lie here,
All of my body tense to the touch of fear,
And my mind,

Muffled now as if the nerves
Refused any longer to let thoughts form,
Is no longer a safe retreat, a tidy home,
No longer serves

My body's demands or shields
With fine words, as it once would daily,
My storehouse of dread. Now, slowly,
My heart, hand, whole body yield

To fear. Bed, ward, window begin
To lose their solidity. Faces no longer
Look kind or needed; yet I still fight the stronger
Terror—oblivion—the needle thrusts in.

II. THE WARD

One with the photographs of grandchildren,
Another with discussion of disease,

Another with the memory of her garden,
Another with her marriage—all of these

Keep death at bay by building round their illness
A past they never honoured at the time.

The sun streams through the window, the earth heaves
Gently for this new season. Blossoms climb

Out in the healthy world where no one thinks
Of pain. Nor would these patients wish them to;

The great preservers here are little things—
The dream last night, a photograph, a view.

III. AFTER AN OPERATION

What to say first? I learnt I was afraid,
Not frightened in the way that I had been
When wideawake and well. I simply mean
Fear became absolute and I became
Subject to it; it beckoned, I obeyed.

Fear which before had been particular,
Attached to this or that scene, word, event,
Here became general. Past, future meant
Nothing. Only the present moment bore
This huge, vague fear, this wish for nothing more.

Yet life still stirred and nerves themselves became
Like shoots which hurt while growing, sensitive
To find not death but further ways to live.
And now I'm convalescent, fear can claim
No general power. Yet I am not the same.

IV. THE VISITORS

They visit me and I attempt to keep
A social smile upon my face. Even here
Some ceremony is required, no deep
Relationship, simply a way to clear
    Emotion to one side; the fear
I felt last night is buried in drugged sleep.

They come and all their kindness makes me want
To cry (they say the sick weep easily).
When they have gone I shall be limp and faint,
My heart will thump and stumble crazily;
    Yet through my illness I can see
One wish stand clear no pain, no fear can taint.

Your absence has been stronger than all pain
And I am glad to find that when most weak
Always my mind returned to you again.
Through all the noisy nights when, harsh awake,
    I longed for day and light to break—
In that sick desert, you were life, were rain.

V. FOR A WOMAN WITH A FATAL ILLNESS

The verdict has been given and you lie quietly
Beyond hope, hate, revenge, even self-pity.

You accept gratefully the gifts—flowers, fruit—
Clumsily offered now that your visitors too

Know you must certainly die in a matter of months.
They are dumb now, reduced only to gestures,

Helpless before your news, perhaps hating
You because you are the cause of their unease.

I too, watching from my temporary corner,
Feel impotent and wish for something violent—

Whether as sympathy only, I am not sure—
But something at least to break the terrible tension.

Death has no right to come so quietly.

Richard Kell

MICROCOSM

Seen as a wilderness
The vegetable patch
Is far from dud:
Let loose, the children scratch
In hollows of dry mud,
Ride on a plank, or watch
The insects in the grass,
Their bodies edged with light,
The tall weeds luminous.

No more than we deserve:
They to be left alone
To play, and I to work
In this clean living-room
Their mother keeps so well:
Routines we may not shirk
Or barely stay alive;
With skill we buy the freedom
That disciplines our skill.

Too young to think it out,
How could they know that we
Who sometimes nag and shout
Are free when they are free,
Clear of the mean restraint
Grafted in all of us.
'Keep out of range', I'd say;
'Let me be generous'.
And they'd wonder what I meant.

James Kirkup

BACKWARDS AND FORWARDS

In the muddle of life and light
We begin to ride slowly backwards
With a going quick as life,
Backwards into the night of birth and breath,
Life's daylight death.

We are those amorous travellers
At night in the coupling express
Who cannot sleep, but only close their eyes,
At no set signal entering the dream
Of travelling backwards in the bucking steam.

But not quite so. Rather
The opposite of that recurrent change:
We go not backwards, but forwards another way.
No matter whether the traveller has got
His back to the locomotive or not.

It only requires an opening of the eyes
A second, to catch the siding lights
Of village halts and country stars
To bring us to ourselves, out of the back
Of beyond, to locomotion's unprogressive track.

While we regret the regressive dream
Of travelling backwards, a drugged suspense
That lets us be at once ahead and far behind,
But always shunted backwards, into the birth
Of death, the present's junction with an infinite of earth.

Until our iron steed soars on for good and all,
And the eyes that were only resting
No longer open. We let our huge godhead go
With ball-bearing abandonment, erect, and in dumb
Spasms elaborately come and come.

Screwing the infinite's hilarious thighs,
The night-soiling stars' hot torrents of sperm
Shot from the trousers of time, a sunburst crotch,
Impregnate the impregnable, our dream's pleasure,
Some unwilling traveller's most private treasure.

With black-oiled piston and barrelled shaft
Torn steams of prayer ransack a tunnel's hole.
—Whoops! This backward movement cannot be
Arrested, reverses clutchless to a forward flight
To miss, and catch, a through-train, the last tonight.

James Kirkup

LAST INSTRUCTIONS

Beat no muffled drum,
No garlands bear.
Let no funerals and monuments of grief
Declare to some
I had recovered from my unbelief.

Come not near my grave
Until you come
As I shall, casting no shadow on that coast
Whose drowning wave
Is no more darkened by life's vivid ghost.

Let dear friends and foes
Wait for my death
To write their customary elegiacs.
Death, decompose
Their compositions with profounder works!

Life was not, and was
My own. Death too
Will be, and not be mine. I shall be deep
Enough to live death's ways,
Learn without memory of love or sleep.

I have survived life
To live death through.
Let no resurrection stone be moved for me.
Let me alive
In the dark wave. Death has its own life too.

B. C. Leale

STUFFED BIRD

In this brittle, charred bird-haunt
Nothing has stirred for half a century,
There have been no seed-case explosions
Or further barbed entanglements of bramble.

Nothing to spring a twig or jolt mould
From a perilous ledge, all remains
Precarious as on the first day of creation—
A matrix for the bird.

No brown common garden bird
But kingfisher—outspread, sapphire-winged,
Flame-bodied, claws to a branch wired—
Feigning the impermanence of flight.

But being rooted and dead, endures
Under a glass sky, stares
Through his beads upon
Our short mortal struttings,

Fierce gaudy flittings
Across time,
Being preserved against the air
And weathers that distress

(Bird-prints about tired eyes)
Our own plummeting lives—
Brittle, charred and haunted
That half a century has not stirred.

B. C. Leale

FAMILY PORTRAIT

Only a photograph preserves them now
With the look of happiness, and the background—
The ancestral house dark with furniture—
Marooned on sharp declines of the eroding future.

Elderly mother and father in innocent Sunday finery
Gaze between son and daughter so photogenically
Filial in affection, that a neighbour in for dinner
Can't see the knife for the cheese.

These elderly children run here and there with
Sheets and blankets, tucking in their lives
Around their parents—a photohappy smile gives
Nothing away but teeth.

Nothing is given away though parents die,
China cannot be smashed or books lost
Or grass be left to overgrow their graves—
Though brother and sister divide themselves
With rooms now cast up from the past,
Encrusted thick with furniture.

Oonagh Lahr

THE ADVANCE ON THE RETREAT

When the city had passed me, my feet took a course that was
  gentle
To a field that was empty, and full of the colour of green
Spread with remembrance, enamelled with various liking
Where even the ditches are clear enough trenched to be trusted
The hedgerows grow neatly, and cleanly the gate hangs on
  hinges
In order so careful it leaves no location for longing.

The city was daunting, and tortured with hope and with longing
The barkers were fierce there, and slopes too afraid to be
  gentle
The arches were falling, and every door shrieked on its hinges.
To relief of staccato, this world here's a cadence of green
The footing of silence on turf makes a pace to be trusted
While the grass has the ease and the spring of immediate liking.

The buttercups shine like small suns of intemperate liking
Which eat up the eye and yet manage to discipline longing
Fulfilling all promise of riches with gold to be trusted
They gladly and smugly reflect back a light that is gentle
And even their scissor-torn leaves are a sureness of green:
The soil of this meadow is scented, the air moves on hinges.

The way to the meadow is easy, there's oil on the hinges
The only requisite is: giving up loving for liking.
And yet of all colours I fear most this marvellous green
A colour that harms you and cheats you with satisfied longing
With turning a passion that's fierce to a kindness that's gentle
(If the kindness of lovers were ever the kind to be trusted).

The cry of the city was: only despair can be trusted,
A point is well-taken when reason is shorn off its hinges,

And levity grows in a field which is sunny and gentle.
The days trickle past and at length I am stifled with liking
I seek for an answer which never can answer my longing
To mow with a sickle that's sharper than this tender green.

By staring at scarlet you find it's the obverse of green.
Look here and away, and which is the hue to be trusted?
To feed on bright scarlet with never a hope of belonging
You batter your head on a door without handle or hinges.
The entry to either recourse is too dear for my liking:
When wishhorses couple with nightmares they breed nothing
gentle.

This tells me that gentleness is not the nature of green.
When I proffer my liking I know that it should be distrusted.
All blame but my own comes from hinging my loving on
longing.

Philip Larkin

NOTHING TO BE SAID

For nations vague as weed,
For nomads among stones,
Small-statured cross-faced tribes
And cobble-close families
In mill-towns on dark mornings,
Life is slow dying.

So are their separate ways
Of building, benediction,
Measuring love and money
Ways of slow dying.
The day spent hunting pig
Or holding a garden-party,

Hours giving evidence
Or birth, advance
On death equally slowly.
And saying so to some
Means nothing; others it leaves
Nothing to be said.

John Lehmann

TELL ME YOUR NAME

Below them, in the street, the linden shook
Raindrops, in sudden pelting, to the ground,
Splashing the hollows in the stones, reflecting
The broken moonglow of the lamp.
But the rain had finished, the cloud birds took
A northward course, warm winds directing.
Across their open window came
The smell of leaves, fresh, damp.

One said: tell me your name.
Why were you standing there alone?
Tomorrow, even, I had planned my train,
But on the bridge I turned, I saw
The slow derisive offer of your mouth.
I had friends waiting, a light heart again,
I was impatient for the lakes, the south;
Now all that's dropped and gone.

Now, as I lean towards your face,
A diver watching the wave smile, so soon
To leap to him, engulf, caress,
I think, still poised—this place
I fix with a falling gesture, I press,
Pressing your lips, a signet in my life,
Imprint deep, deep, this moon, this lamp,
And from the linden, after storm in June,
The smell of leaves, fresh, damp.

George MacBeth

'THE SPIDER'S NEST

Was clenched on a fly's carcass like a golden
Fist which exploded into an abacus
Of excited beads at the prick of my quill'

Is one verse. 'This morning I arranged about
A hundred things with legs on invisible
Wires to dance attendance' is another. To

Be crippled and have such tensed will subdued by
A feather pleases. On a wheeled bed or an
Orbed web life rakes old sores over with my (or

Some other) tough hand. The feather of death in
One's bowels tickles the triumph out of such
Teasing of puissance. Day after day to lie

Here watching the sun skate in the sky, wanting
Death but unable to move except enough
To kill wasps with a book or annoy spiders

Is something. After all, success in drowning
Ants in vermouth requires only time and I
Collect it like dust. Snakes come. Visitors with

French sonnets. Minestrone for supper. Floods
In May. If Stock insists on a third verse I
Suggest 'a few hesitated between the

Abrupt brink of air and the known centre of
A gauze mesh where their inherited fly lay
Spread out to be eaten' but I'm not keen on

A fourth verse. To leave great themes unfinished is
Perhaps the most satisfying exercise
Of power. Describing their look of being

The armour of a god left hanging overnight in a skein of frost can be decently
Left to Vernon. Sleep comes. And with it my snails.

Florence, 1885, Eugene Lee-Hamilton

George MacBeth

BOREDOM

Somewhere (yes, I know where,
No, I won't tell you where)
Well-fed, warm and at ease
Lying late in a bed
Out of a window I
Watch a dead station-wall.
Scene one: nothing, as yet.

Next, through wet streets I walk,
Rinsed out after the rain.
Someone (no, I don't know
Who, but only her—yes)
Walks in front of me, well
Wrapped up after the rain.
Scene two: all right, you win.

Somehow (well, you know how,
You've been there in your time)
Women's fingers that lock
Lock and lock and lock. Well,
Then, upstairs to a room
Bang up against a wall.
Scene three: back as you were.

Scene four: (is there a fourth?
No, it just peters out).
Why does every affair
Sometimes (looking around
One's life) seem to involve
Just the same station wall
Seen from bed in the rain?

R. S. Morgan

DIVERTIMENTO XIX

Like vertical crusaders, oaves
Stand on crossed legs. All trelliswork
    Looks temporary.
But boredom and the cabbagerose
Keep one foot in the grave and smirk
    At the antiquary.

Numa Clive Negri

ON THE ISLAND

Grey dawns and bursting spray. Sandra laughing in the wind.
The house fresh painted. Marvin sowing rye.
Sweet rain water on young buds; cattle at the pool.
Tracks in the sand; white linen on the line:
And the steamer due within a month.

The high crop standing and the rocks warm
In the sun. Marianne all blowzy in the heat.
Michael clearing timber on the hill. Flies above the pool.
Arid nights, and every dawn a forest fire
With the whole of Africa inverted in the sky.

Summer drawn to a tremendous close.
The boat pulled up beyond the tide. Sandra
Going off alone. The house so dark
In shutters to the east. Michael sombre,
Talking now of Catalina, Marvin of the fuel
Lost from the beach. Lanterns light the barn.
Night wind and the passage of time.

Sandra's weeping. Marvin's swearing. The gull's cry
From the headland. The colour of the soil; Michael
Threatening to leave; the others pleading.
Snow in the wind. Then Marvin dead,
Spindrift on the shore,
And Marianne with child.

Hubert Nicholson

THE BONFIRE

Its petals brighten as dusk deepens
The bonfire ringed with apple trees
With boughs where moss clings like the dusk
Daffodils seem at first to brighten too
But dusk, that flatters them, as velvet gold, as firelight girls,
Will quench them in the end.
The bonfire dies, grows; lights on children darting from the trees
To leap about it; in whose mirror eyes
Small petals leap. My own senses quicken
In the to-fro of yellows, catch the flame
But on the surface only; in my deep depths all is still
Where opens, cool and slow, a memory,
Print of some other blaze and flower,
Laid down in some such hour and carrying
Calm assurance of love, no longer mine;
So for the children this may that moment be
To be relit at such another time
When they will stand where I stand now:
Or will oblivion take it and dusk drown it,
And will it go, when I go, where I go?

Kathleen Nott

VOUS, HYPOCRITE LECTEUR . . .

(A Fable)

A crocodile
up to the bulbous eyes
she could not lower from contemplation of the skies
was basking in the solid-squalid reaches
of some river, no doubt, the Nile;
training invisible, but most likely of the Estuarine sub-species
(which would not be despised by their colossal
forbears, only found in fossil,
and gigantic): and with comparable capacity
to those long still,
living in an appetite of unsurpassed voracity.

This article which looks so cumbersome and is so agile
is a dead loss in and around and on the Nile;
Pluvianus even, (aegyptius)—kind of plover—
which plucks the parasites from her gaping head,
is symbiotic but no lover,
or cannot tell her patience, perhaps gratitude, from being
dead.

And yet she has her virtues. Abstract, strictly formal
(as if the daedal, all-foreknowing God,
forereading Jeans: and with intention of designing
a geometric, that is, self-defining
shape, like sphere or rhomboid, cube or square,
made her perhaps too normal)
at least she is not odd,
with the blowzy and eccentric features
of most incalculable creatures,
but like an axiom she is always *there*.

And is it not virtue—to consubstantiate
oneself with Time? For Patience is a virtue
whose deeds are strung upon the infinite:
and so before the Judgement closes daylight,
take their place, before death, enough of courage and a trace
of truth and love: for who can wait
at all, can wait for ever.

And this long Rule of Silence in the river
raucous and unsightly with her foes,
as between the littoral and the flood,
among morbid vegetation and the pestilential leeches,
in this belt of cowardly torturers she beaches
her proboscis, un-
nictitating under the unwinking sun,
may feel, for all one knows,
along her blue-cold antediluvian blood,
pride in her ancient craft of rigor and her intimate armour:
and, like a perfect emblem, she
teaches the last virtue, of Necessity,
to all too stiff to run,
the dignity of dying for livelihood, not glory.

And even supposing it is true
that some cacophonous hullaballoo
seizes her from time to time, and bellowing clamour,
might not this confirm the other and unlikely story
which I now repeat? that she was smartly smitten
by quite unprecedented lacrimosity?

Those standing wells of vision which abode
as immemorially upon her head
suddenly overflowed
and spilled by each minute rugosity
to join the turgid waste of waters where it stank and spread.

Much (and much mendacious) has been written
the crocodile had not read

(indeed how can you read with eyes in that position)
about the incidence of this condition:
anyway she was not cribbing; it appears,
deep in floods which she augmented with those tears,
like a long-lost and once-beleaguered city,
something moved her pity, or self-pity,
to weeping old and deep and real as would have been
our strange weeping when we weep alone.

For only then our grief
is like Leviathan passing
at leagues of inner distance,
and maybe even for coral depths and waste of years.
Seeing her, we would have seen
(not like one who tries
to catch love as sundew flies)
her at her private soul, while on that hideous head those
flawless tears
like a poem suspended disbelief,
and reflected on the strangeness of our own:
tears, any tears, we know not what they mean.

But suppose she *knew*, who cannot speak,
would not that moment be
phylogenetically unique,
when silence old as light
went straight as flight towards a wall of all our nature
no one could foresee?

As if whole and other lobes
broke once from low amoebal mud,
and those twin and bitter lobes
every internecine creature
needs double and apart,
broke inwards to a single heart,
and every black box into bud?

Mervyn Peake

GREAT HULK DOWN THE ASTONISHED WATERS DRIFTING . . .

Great hulk down the astonished waters drifting:
Hulk of green crust the ocean birds disdain:
I hear her mutter that the pain is shifting.

See where the dolphins shall not sport again:
There drifts the hulk: the seaweed round her throat
A dripping necklace thicker than a mane

And cold as loneliness. She is afloat
On heavy water, wallowing like those
That rock themselves for comfort in remote

Corners of wards, or when the anguish grows
Curl up like hedgehogs when the light is raw
Great hulk of love, how thick the water flows.

Where is her captain and the famous shore
Where danced the golden sailors? Where's the sea
That sang of water when the heart was free
And mermaids swam where mermaids swim no more?

Sylvia Plath

THE MOON AND THE YEW TREE

This is the light of the mind, cold and planetary.
The trees of the mind are black. The light is blue.
The grasses unload their griefs on my feet as if I were God,
Prickling my ankles and murmuring of their humility.
Fumey, spiritous mists inhabit this place
Separated from my house by a row of headstones.
I simply cannot see where there is to get to.

The moon is no door. It is a face in its own right,
White as a knuckle and terribly upset.
It drags the sea after it like a dark crime; it is quiet
With the O-gape of complete despair. I live here.
Twice on Sunday, the bells startle the sky—
Eight great tongues affirming the Resurrection.
At the end, they soberly bong out their names.

The yew tree points up. It has a Gothic shape.
The eyes lift after it and find the moon.
The moon is my mother. She is not sweet like Mary.
Her blue garments unloose small bats and owls.
How I would like to believe in tenderness!——
The face of the effigy, gentled by candles,
Bending, on me in particular, its mild eyes.

I have fallen a long way. Clouds are flowering
Blue and mystical over the face of the stars.
Inside the church, the saints will be all blue,
Floating on their delicate feet over the cold pews,
Their hands and faces stiff with holiness.
The moon sees nothing of this. She is bald and wild.
And the message of the yew trees is blackness—blackness and
silence.

Sylvia Plath

TULIPS

The tulips are too excitable, it is winter here.
Look how white everything is, how quiet, how snowed-in.
I am learning peacefulness, lying by myself quietly
As the light lies on these white walls, this bed, these hands.
I am nobody; I have nothing to do with explosions.
I have given my name and my day-clothes up to the nurses
And my history to the anæsthetist and my body to surgeons.

They have propped my head between the pillow and the
sheet-cuff
Like an eye between two white lids that will not shut.
Stupid pupil, it has to take everything in.
The nurses pass and pass, they are no trouble,
They pass the way gulls pass inland in their white caps,
Doing things with their hands, one just the same as another,
So it is impossible to tell how many there are.

My body is a pebble to them, they tend it as water
Tends to the pebbles it must run over, smoothing them gently.
They bring me numbness in their bright needles, they bring
me sleep.
Now I have lost myself I am sick of baggage—
My patent leather overnight case like a black pillbox,
My husband and child smiling out of the family photo;
Their smiles catch on to my skin, little smiling hooks.

I have let things slip, a thirty-year-old cargo boat
Stubbornly hanging on to my name and address.
They have swabbed me clear of my loving associations.
Scared and bare on the green plastic-pillowed trolley
I watched my teaset, my bureau of linen, my books
Sink out of sight, and the water went over my head.
I am a nun now, I have never been so pure.

I didn't want any flowers, I only wanted
To lie with my hands turned up and be utterly empty.
How free it is, you have no idea how free—
The peacefulness is so big it dazes you,
And it asks nothing, a name tag, a few trinkets.
It is what the dead close on, finally; I imagine them
Shutting their mouths on it, like a Communion tablet.

The tulips are too red in the first place, they hurt me.
Even through the gift paper I could hear them breathe
Lightly, through their white swaddlings, like an awful baby.
Their redness talks to my wound, it corresponds.
They are subtle: they seem to float, though they weigh me
down,
Upsetting me with their sudden tongues and their colour,
A dozen red lead sinkers round my neck.

Nobody watched me before, now I am watched.
The tulips turn to me, and the window behind me
Where once a day the light slowly widens and slowly thins,
And I see myself, flat, ridiculous, a cut-paper shadow
Between the eye of the sun and the eyes of the tulips,
And I have no face, I have wanted to efface myself.
The vivid tulips eat my oxygen.

Before they came the air was calm enough,
Coming and going, breath by breath, without any fuss.
Then the tulips filled it up like a loud noise.
Now the air snags and eddies round them the way a river
Snags and eddies round a sunken rust-red engine.
They concentrate my attention, that was happy
Playing and resting without committing itself.

The walls, also, seem to be warming themselves.
The tulips should be behind bars like dangerous animals;
They are opening like the mouth of some great African cat,
And I am aware of my heart: it opens and closes
Its bowl of red blooms out of sheer love of me.
The water I taste is warm and salt, like the sea,
And comes from a country far away as health.

Peter Redgrove

SHE GHOSTS . . .

She ghosts that firm white cigarette in sips;
The dress fades over her throat in puffs
Of tulle; she thrusts the window wide;
Earth turns into the pre-dawn light;
From the chimney-stacks the white smoke-ghosts
Begin, rooted and running.

An ashtray falls to the floor with a ring,
Spurts grey ashes, erasing in the breeze;
Her martini shivers,
Sobs spirit up the sides in rings;
She thrusts her eyes wide into the chill; with tears
The white breath-ghost goes,
Rooted and running.

The party's smokes fade in chill.
I cross, and pull the window close, take
Her warmth into my own, for the white breath-ghosts:
Since we are not dawn spiralling into the air,
Nor earth in her dew-sweat, nor fevered grass
Rooted and running, yet.

Peter Redgrove

THE SWARM

A community of flies sleets my pane
Nipped at the waist in shiny jacketing,
Commas, helmeted with heads: the too-abundant kind
That swarms in packs through coastal towns and walks,
Get slopped on fields in whirring bucketfuls.
They reek their buzz; I roll my paper tight;
My eye slips through their whizzing to the street. . . .

Laced, like silhouettes in shiny jacketing,
Skull-domed boys leap across their saddles,
Goggling sockets stern, and in a swarm
Shout their motor-bikes along these walls,
Variations on the syllable aaah of power,
Dwindling to a honeyed buzz. Sleet up the hill
To sate on writhing passages of scenery,
While my paper hesitates, as the kerb can swat,
Holds off, white edges dip and sweep.

Christopher Scaife

GARDEN TOMBS

In moonlit nights some died,
and others when the moon went down,
and some when, turning like the tide,
the first dawn makes a black leaf brown;
some few at noon,
and many when the cooking-pots beside
the fire at evening shone.

Though some were brought too soon,—
young, virginal, not half awake,—
and others, like the waning moon,
lingered and lingered, till daybreak
showed them as ghosts,
yet like a solved acrostic or a rune
these gardens were to most.

This tomb, half-hidden, boasts
a rose that flowers all the year;
this, cracked, with slanting lintel-posts,
has cypress-shade; on that one there
the iris grows,
trooping the unfurled standards of its hosts
in honourable show.

Which of us living knows
they erred, (who laid their fellows thus),
thinking the first of men uprose
from garden-ground—and fathered us—
though now we plan
a self-sufficient, man-made world which flows
not from God through Adam?

However things began,
we say, God, like the gods, was made,
by us, for garden-walks, we cannot use them on the autostrade—
        and are too proud
to see that, perhaps, god created man
   and by Man invents God.

Vernon Scannell

SUICIDE

Alone, he came to his decision,
The sore tears stiffening his cheeks
As headlamps flicked the ceiling with white dusters
And darkness roared downhill with nervous brakes.
Below, the murmuring and laughter,
The baritone, tobacco-smelling jokes;
And then his misery and anger
Suddenly became articulate:
'I wish that I was dead. Oh, they'll be sorry then!
I hate them and I'll kill myself tomorrow.
I want to die. I hate them, hate them. Hate.'

And kill himself in fact he did,
But not next day as he'd decided.
The deed itself, for thirty years deferred,
Occurred one wintry night when he was loaded.
Belching with scotch and misery
He turned the gas tap on and placed his head
Gently, like a pudding, in the oven.
'I want to die. I'll hurt them yet,' he said,
And once again: 'I hate them, hate them. Hate.'
The lampless darkness roared inside his skull
Then sighed into a silence in which played
The grown up voices, still up late,
Indifferent to his rage as to his fate.

Edith Sitwell

'HIS BLOOD COLOURS MY CHEEK'

A saying of St Agnes

(For The Very Rev. M. C. D'Arcy, S.J., LL.D., D.Litt., Litt.D., F.R.S.L.)

His Blood colours my cheek.
Ah! Were but those Flames the tongue wherewith I speak
Of the small ambitions I have seen
Rise in the common street
Where the bell that tolls in Bedlam tolls the hour.
Yet still great flowers like violet thunders break
In air, and still the flower of the five-petalled senses
Is surely ours.
I, an old dying woman, tied
To the winter's hopelessness
And to a wisp of bone
Clothed in the old world's outworn foolishness
—A poor Ape-cerement
With all its rags of songs, loves, rages, lusts, and flags of death
Say this to you,
My father Pithecanthropus Erectus, your head once filled with
 primal night,
You who stood at last after the long centuries
Of the anguish of the bone
Reaching upward towards the loving, the all-understanding
 sun—
To you, who no more walk on all fours like the first
Gardener and grave-digger, yet are listening
Where, born from zero, little childish leaves and lives begin!
I hear from the dust the small ambitions rise.
The White Ant whispers: 'Could I be Man's size,

My cylinders would stretch three hundred feet
In air, and Man would look at me with different eyes!'

And there the Brazilian insect all day long
Challenges the heat with its heavy noise:
'Were I as great as Man, my puny voice
Would stretch from Pole to Pole, no other sound
Be audible. By this dictatorship the round
World would be challenged—from my uproar would a new
Civilization of the dust be born, the old world die like dew.'
I watch the new world of rulers, the snub-nosed,[1] the vain, and
the four-handed,[2]
Building a new Babel for the weak
Who walk with the certainty of the somnambulist
Upon the tight-rope stretched over nothingness—
Holding a comet and the small ape-dust in their fist
Over the grave where the heart of Man is laid.
I hear the empty straw whine to the street
Of the ghost that has no bread, the lonely ghost
That lacks prosperity: 'I am your Wheat:
Come and be fed!'
But I see the sun, large as the journeying foot of Man, see the
great traveller
Fearing no setting, going straight to his destination,
So am I not dismayed.
His Blood colours my cheek;—
No more eroded by the seas of the world's passions and greeds,
I rise
As if I never had been ape, to look in the compassionate, the all-
seeing Eyes.

1. 'According to a statement of an ancient Chinese work of about 2000 B.C. a so-called man of the Hen Yeung Kingdom appears from his up-turned nose to be a snub-nosed monkey' (Rhinopithicus).—*Man As An Animal.* W. C. Osman Hill, M.D., F.R.S.E. (Hutchinson University Library).

2. 'At one time, it was indeed the practice, in spite of their recognized and obvious connection with man, for apes and monkeys to be called Quadramana, or four-handed ones (and) to relegate man to a separate order called Bimania (i.e. two-handed).'—*Op. cit.*

Edith Sitwell

THE WAR ORPHANS

(Written after seeing a photograph of Korean children asleep in the snow)

The snow is the blood of these poor Dead . . . they have no
 other—
These children, old in the dog's scale of years, too old
For the hopeless breast—ghosts for whom there is none to care,
Grown fleshless as the skeleton
Of Adam, they have known
More aeons of the cold than he endured
In the first grave of the world. They have, for bed,
The paving stones, the spider spins their blankets, and their
 bread
Is the shred and crumb of dead Chance. In this epoch of the
 cold,
In which new worlds are formed, new glaciations
To overcast the world that was the heart,
There is only that architecture of the winter, the huge plan
Of the lasting skeleton, built from the hunger of Man,
Constructed for hunger—piteous in its griefs, the humiliation
Of outworn flesh, the ape-cerement, O the foolish tattered
 clothing,
Rags stained with the filth of humanity, stink of its toiling,
But never the smell of the heart, with its warmth, its fevers,
Rapacity and grandeur. For the cold is zero
In infinite intensity, brother to democratic
Death, our one equality, who holds
Alike the maelstrom of the blood, the world's incendiarism,
The summer redness and the hope of the rose
The beast, and man's superiority o'er the beast
That is but this:
Man bites with his smile, and poisons with his kiss.
When, in each dawn,

The light on my brow is changed to the mark of Cain,
And my blood cries 'Am I my brother's keeper?' seeing these
    ghosts
Of Man's forgetfulness of Man, I feel again
The pitiless but healing rain—who thought I only
Had the lonely Lethe flood for tears.

Stephen Spender

THE GENEROUS DAYS

(Aetat 18)

His are the generous days that balance
Soul and body. Should he hear the trumpet
Behind the sun that sends its thinning ray
Penetrating to the marrow—
At once one with that cause, he'd throw
Himself across some high far parapet,
Body die to soul down the sheer way
Of consummation in the summons.

His also are the days when should he greet
Her who goes walking, looking for a brooch
Under broad leaves at dusk beside the path
—And sidelong looks at him as though she thought
His smile might hide the gleam she sought—
He would run up to her and each
Find the lost clasp hid in them both,
Soul live to body where they meet.

Body soul, soul body, seem one breath,
Or the twined shadows of the sun, his will,
In these his generous days, to prove
His own true nature only is to give.
Wholly to die, or wholly else to live!
Body to soul, and let the bright cause kill,
Or soul to body, let the blood make love.
Giving is death in life and life in death.

After, of course, will come a time not this
When he'll be taken, stripped, strapped to a wheel
That is a world, and has the power to change
The brooch's gold, the trumpet scarlet blaze

—The lightning in the bones those generous days—
Into what drives a system, like a fuel.
Then to himself he will seem loathed and strange
Have thoughts yet colder than the thing he is.

Jon Silkin

THE DISTRACTION

(For Ian Hamilton)

Yesterday
She gathered flowers into
Her arms; and though I cannot
Tell you what the life
Was named, I know that these
Were last flowers; some final
Intermission of colour
Before the season falls.
So that in this poise
In which a woman took
A mortal thing to her
There seemed a poignancy;
As though the figure of
Proserpine near Dis
Breathed into that bent form;
One flower entering
Another at her breast.
And all the time she gathered
The fairest delicacy
The dead nourish in nature
Not for man's delight but
For the whole exacting process
Of growth towards the earth.
Yet from the earth
Some pincering insect form
Emerged, as if it would
Draw them and death below;
As though winter did not
Contract the spines of life
Closely enough to death.

Edward Lucie-Smith

RUBENS PAINTS HELENE FOURMENT

(*The picture is* La Pelisse, *now in Vienna*)

Now sinking towards age, I paint your rising.
Your flesh glows with my sunset. You wrap close
A dark fur robe, which clothes and half unclothes you.
Each little movement brushes the rich texture
Against thigh, buttock, breast. And now I serve
More fiercely than I did our wedding night
Your pearly substance. Dear, I know too well
What you in your turn see: a florid statesman
Burdened with excess of fame. If the long years
Instruct me now in fusing tone with tone
Until the painted you seems made of flowers,
My skill is nothing to you—just the years.

You bring a sort of love
To meet my love. I know that all I've taught
Your lovely body in our linen sheets
Would run at once to meet me if I touched you.
But when I go?—I see you plan already.
Good Flemish thoughts stir in those aqueous eyes
Of what a rich young widow, fertile (see
The proof of healthy children) can expect.
Whom will you choose to reap my benefits?
A noble? Young? A warrior? Look, Helene—
My pictures give a blessing. The hard steel
A hero's clad in many a time reflects
Like bonfires in its depth, the rosy sheen
Of woman armoured just as you are now.

And yet I win:
I paint this picture. No one will remember
Another man has owned you. Everyone
Will see you thus, in the act of being possessed

More coarsely, more completely than in all
The many separate times I came to take you.

I chose well. And I chose. It was not folly,
A doddering, mumbling, stupid lickerishness,
Made me pick you. I might have married nobly,
But nothing so noble as this youthful body.
I find more meaning here than I've discovered
In all the allegories my patrons set me.
My lust cried for you. But love, too, for the race,
The female richness. I can hardly tell
Sometimes on waking whether I have dreamt
Of walking slowly near my tower of Steen
The fields I own, the hedgepaths, or if I
Have simply strolled about that rich estate,
Helene's young body. Why do these, the blue
Veins by your neck, the lesser pearls
Circling the large pearl in your flowering nipples,
Even the feet, cramped by fine shoes I gave you,
Seem more like landmarks that the marks we set
To show where Steen's fields march beside a neighbour's?
I feed upon you, warm my hands before you,
You ward the rains off, bring me government
(The hand governs the brush, the mind the hand,
The mind's discipline is to re-create you).
Your flesh springs from that dark robe like a rainbow
Bursting a cloud, and is as full of promise.

Sometimes, these nights, a wild hunt fills my dream:
A lioness, impaled, that tries to reach me
Up to my stout spearshaft. Then the high-pitched clamour
Of fallen men and claw-raked stallions screaming
Is muted to a buzz, and leaning down
Out of the saddle as my horse rears skyward
I see, moving small and clear with the tawny
Crystal of eyes, your double image—silks
And golden tresses. And I wake to find
You move beneath me like a lioness,

Silken and supple, naked in our bed,
Face veiled beneath a golden fall of hair.

I pass you on in entail. They inherit
Who learn to look. I leave you to be hunted
By other appetites. I cannot help
But bring my nature to your natural good.
I set all down, and sign you: RUBENS PINXIT.

Stevie Smith

THE LAST TURN OF THE SCREW

I am Miles, I did not die
I only turned as on shut eye
To feel again the silken dress
Of my lovely governess.

Yes, it was warm, poetical, and cosy,
I never saw the other fellow when
I lolled on Lady's lap (I called her Lady)
But there were two of us all right. And both were men.

Yes, there's the oddest part. She made me feel
A hundred years more old than I was, than she was,
She'd had a sheltered life, of course, a vicarage,
Some bustling younger children, a father pious, I'm sure he was.

But two of us? Of me? I'll be explicit,
A soft boy, knowing rather more than boys should, lolling,
No harm in that, on Lady's lap; the other,
Source of my knowledge, half my self by now, but calling . . .

Some children are born innocent, some achieve it,
You scowl, that doesn't fit with your philosophy?
Can you by choosing alter Nature, you inquire?
Yes, my dear sir, you can; I found it fairly easy.

But calling (to go back a step) but calling?—
That proved he was not yet quite One of Us,
The vulgar little beast, the fellow Quint.
It was at first my lordly feelings held him off,
That dapper knowingness of his for instance,
The clothes right, being my uncle's, but worn wrong,
The accent careful, well he must be careful,
I daresay he had thumbed a book about it . . .

To spend ten minutes with a Thing like this
Would be too long.
So snobbery made the breach; religion followed . . .
Ten minutes? No, Eternity, with *Quint*,
This Quint, whose seedy sickness in my blood
I could detect (in time?) running to flood,
The sickliness of sin,
Oh yes, I saw quite plain by now
What was going in.
How did I fob him off? (now we know why)
When half my heart
Was panting for him and what he could teach,
Reaching for shame, and retching too
(It was, as I have said, this squeamishness I had
First judged him bad.)
Oh there was still some rotting to go on
In my own heart
Before I was quite ready to cry 'Out!'
And see him off, though half my blood went with him.
I grow a shade dramatic here, none went at all,
My sinews have remained the same, my blood, my heart
Have not, as I'm aware, taken a taint,
I was not and I am not now a saint,
But I loved Virtue, and I love her still,
Especially as I see her in the dress
Of my sweetly fatheaded governess . . .

Well, let's be plain, I fobbed Quint off
By simply failing to be clever enough,
By taking nothing in, not looking and not noticing
I made myself as dull to the persuading
Of all that shabby innuendo as
The plainest ten-year schoolboy ever was;
And so I have remained, and by intent,
Quite dull. And shall remain
Sooner than chance such entering again.
I did not die, but bought my innocence
At the high price of an indifference

Where once I knew the most engaging love
That first through squeamishness made virtue move,
The love, now lost, of my sweet governess
Who cannot bear I should be so much less
The Miles she knew, or rather did not know.
Yes, I have lost my interestingness for Lady who
I fear, as other innocent ladies do,
Hankered for something shady,
Well, say dramatic, not what I am now,
An empty antic Clumsy, a mere boy.
She'll never know
The strength I have employed and do employ
To make it sure
I shall be this
And nothing more.

I am Miles, I did not die,
I only turn, as on shut eye
To feel again the silken dress
Of my lost and lovely governess,
And sigh and think it strange
That being dull I should feel so much pain.

Stevie Smith

TENUOUS AND PRECARIOUS

Tenuous and Precarious
Were my guardians,
Precarious and Tenuous,
Two Romans.

My father was Hazardous,
Hazardous,
Dear old man,
Three Romans.

There was my brother Spurious,
Spurious Posthumous,
Spurious was Spurious,
Was four Romans.

My husband was Perfidious,
He was Perfidious,
Five Romans.

Surreptitious, our son,
Was Surreptitious,
He was six Romans.

Our cat Tedious
Still lives,
Count not Tedious
Yet.

My name is Finis,
Finis, Finis,
I am Finis,
Six, five, four, three, two,
One Roman,
Finis.

Bernard Spencer

BOAT POEM

I wish there were a touch of these boats about my life;
so to speak a tarring,
the touch of inspired disorder and something more than that,
something more too
than the mobility of sails or a primitive bumpy engine
under that tiny hot-house window,
which eats up oil and benzine perhaps
but will go on beating in spite of the many strains
not needing with luck to be repaired too often,
with luck lasting years piled on years.

There must be a kind of envy which brings me peering
and nosing at the boats along the island quay
either in the hot morning
with the lace-light shaking up against their hulls from the
water,
or when their mast-tops
keep on drawing lines between stars.
(I do not speak here of the private yachts from the clubs
which stalk across the harbour like magnificent white cats
but sheer off and keep mostly to themselves.)

Look for example at the *Bartolomé*; a deck-full
of mineral water and bottles of beer in cases
and great booming barrels of wine from the mainland,
endearing trade;
and lengths of timber and iron rods for building
and, curiously, a pig with flying ears
ramming a wet snout into whatever it explores.

Or the *Virgin del Pilar*, mantled and weavy with drooping nets
PM/708/3A
with starfish and pieces of cod drying on the wheel-house roof

some wine, the remains of supper on an enamel plate
and trousers and singlets 'passim';
both of these boats stinky and forgivable like some great men
both needing paint,
but both, one observes, armoured far better than us against
jolts
by a belt of old motor-tyres lobbed round their sides for buffers.

And having in their swerving planks and in the point of their
bows
the never-enough-to-be-praised
authority of a great tradition, the sea-shape
simple and true like a vase,
something that stays too in the carved head of an eagle
or that white-eyed wooden hound crying up beneath the bow-
sprit.

Qualities clearly admirable. So is their response to occasion,
how they celebrate such times
and suddenly fountain with bunting and stand like ocean
maypoles
on a Saint's Day when a gun bangs from the fortifications,
and an echo-gun throws a bang back
and all the old kitchen bells start hammering from the
churches.

Admirable again
how one of them, perhaps tomorrow, will have gone with no
hooting or fuss,
simply absent from its place among the others,
occupied, without self-importance, in the thousands-of-
millions-of sea.

Derek Stanford

THE LIE-A-WAIT

Across the folding counter, in the shop
they call the Gas Pavilion, stale with gas,
I heard those summer nomads shout and clap
for Dolly Deathtrap—Dolly, Queen of Pop—
toast of the flannelled fops, the sportsmen's doxie.

Lukewarm the ginger-beer and cool the tea
fair deathless Dolly serves the likes of me
and all who pay the price but would not slake
her frantic lust beside the antic lake
after the closing of the Gas Pavilion.

So, with the rites of each returning evening—
those shuttered windows pale with chinks of gas—
seen from afar, the grey pavilion falters,
its walls dissolving in the solid earth,
conveying Dolly to her cryptic Mass.

Thenceforth, by footless passage-ways,
mistress and victim seek that shore
where bone and water bleakly meet,
and breath forsakes the savaged boar
whose tusks no longer grace the Gas Pavilion:

Get cracking, Dolly; they can't wait all night.

John Heath-Stubbs

COMMUNICATIONS

With the philosophers in their beleagured city,
Besieged by warlock words,
Drinking the last dregs
From the central well, until
There is nothing left to drink,
Excepting of course hemlock:

With the scientists shoving their eyebrows
Into the excrement, studying
Animalculae and atoms
Through the wrong end of a micro-telescope,
Besieged by gibbering, non-factual ghosts:

With the poets writhing as they chew
Their last scrap of toxic laurel,
Besieged by verbal whores
And the usual poetry-lovers:

With the politicians dreaming of geometry,
Besieged by faceless men;
And the mathematicians dreaming of justice,
Besieged by infinity;
Each of them wondering whether their separate game
Is truly worth the candle:

With the theologians lighting that candle,
Before they collapse, at the foot of the altar,
Dumb oxen, stupefied by glory,
Besieged by the single and real
Little devil of doubt—
'And you won't give me money I'll sweep you all out!'

With everyone else, stuck
In front of the blind television set
Or the radio which breaks down
In the middle of an announcement—merely
That the world is about to come to an end—
Besieged by boredom and commonplace death:

With these what communication?—Unless
The courteous angel comes and goes
In diplomatic immunity,
With authority to reconstitute a fragmented empire,
Delivering code messages
To which the cipher has been lost:
Conjectured to read 'Love'—
Itself a meaningless word.

Anthony Thwaite

SICK CHILD

Lit by the small night-light you lie
And look through swollen eyes at me:
Vulnerable, sleepless, try
To stare through a blank misery,
And now that boisterous creature I
Have known so often shrinks to this
Wan ghost unsweetened by my kiss.

Shaken with retching, bewildered by
The virus curdling milk and food,
You do not scream in fear, or cry.
Tears are another thing, a mood
Given an image, infancy
Making permitted show of force,
Boredom, or sudden pain. The source

Of this still vacancy's elsewhere.
Like my sick dog, ten years ago,
Who skulked away to some quiet lair
With poison in her blood: you know
Her gentleness, her clouded stare,
Pluck blankets as she scratched the ground.
She made, and you now make, no sound.

The rank smell shrouds you like a sheet.
Tomorrow we must let crisp air
Blow through the room and make it sweet,
Making all new. I touch your hair,
Damp where the forehead sweats, and meet—
Here by the door, as I leave you—
A cold, quiet wind, chilling me through.

Anthony Thwaite

THE BOYS

Six of them climbed aboard,
None of them twenty yet,
At a station up the line:
Flannel shirts rimmed with sweat,
Boots bulled to outrageous shine,
Box-pleats stiff as a board.

Pinkly, smelling of Bass,
They lounged on the blue moquette
And rubbed their blanco off.
One told of where to get
The best crumpet. A cough
From the corner. One wrote on the glass

A word in common use.
The others stirred and jeered.
Reveille was idled through
Till the next station appeared,
And the six of them all threw
Their Weights on the floor. Excuse

For a laugh on the platform. Then
We rattled, and moved away,
The boys only just through the door.
It was near the end of the day.
Two slept. One farted and swore,
And went on about his women.

Three hours we had watched this lot,
All of us family men,
Responsible, set in our ways.
I looked at my paper again:
Another H-test. There are days
You wonder whether you're not

Out of touch, old hat, gone stale.
I remembered my twenty-first,
In the NAAFI, laid out cold.
Then one of them blew and burst
A bag; and one of the old
Told them to stow it. The pale

Lights of the city came near.
We drew in and stopped. The six
Bundled their kit and ran.
'A good belting would sort out their tricks',
Said my neighbour, a well-spoken man.
'Yes, but . . .' But he didn't hear.

R. S. Thomas

EH?

Davies said life was long;
There was a sameness in the song.

Pugh thought it all too brief,
The fruit bad before the leaf

Turned. How is it with you,
Who have neither the greed of Pugh

Nor Davies' lack of zest
For the red meat on the breast?

Terence Tiller

CONTINUUM

(*The Cam: 1939–1958*)

Rich bodied stone the small stone bedded stream
preserved and planted green of bank and bough
still honeyed by the fixative sunlight now
as then impassive and unparting now as then
memorial without promise but a theme
an inter-time or turning back again

the scape not undone but by restoration
blazoned anew as the drops change yet not
the stream the dynasties of leaf the plot
of interlacing raining or of light and never
the play the interplay gold celebration
in green white hazel theatres playing forever

on altered flesh the altering hours relight
all scattered waterdrops continuum
of river selves and city of years that come
unparted so repassing echoing and so still
the pictures though they travel yet they write
one manifold in peace of time and will

Terence Tiller

NOTES FOR A MYTH

A hand thrust out of the flames, a feather-slender
white and impossible hand on a delicate arm.
No body, and no burning; still; in form
a girl's: but phantasy or salamander?
Ringless, the wrong shape, dead as alabaster,
it was not like; and yet—oh friend and sister—
by its immune acceptance of the fires,
    I knew the hand was yours.

A hand grew out of the wall, strong-fruiting flesh
more deeply rooted than the brick and plaster;
the fingers flexing; dark; in cruel gesture.
A man's, but huge as pain to seize and crush.
Blunt as an oak-leaf, knotted, bronze as thunder,
it was not like; yet, by the alien grandeur
that gave it empire over mysteries,
    I knew the hand was his.

A hand swam high on the river; slimy lustre,
as if of pearl-shell, silvering its death;
blood on the nails; on the torn wrist a wreath
of withered petals clotted, and a cluster
of drift-weed that would slowly draw it under.
It was not like; yet in that last surrender
I saw the myth and all that it should mean,
    and knew the hand was mine.

Charles Tomlinson

WINTER-PIECE

You wake, all windows blind—embattled sprays
grained on the medieval glass.
Gates snap like gunshot
as you handle them. Five-barred fragility
sets flying fifteen rooks who go together
silently ravenous above this winter-piece
that will not feed them. They alight
beyond, scavenging, missing everything
but the bladed atmosphere, the white resistance.
Ruts with iron flanges track
through a hard decay
where you discern once more
oak-leaf by hawthorn, for the frost
rewhets their edges. In a perfect web
blanched along each spoke
and circle of its woven wheel,
the spider hangs, grasp unbroken
and death-masked in cold. Returning
you see the house glint-out behind
its holed and ragged glaze,
frost-fronds all streaming.

W. Price Turner

INCIDENT IN CITY STREET

When a naked man runs earnestly enough
among shoppers with little problems of their own,
the thread of his passing leaves them in tucks
and wrinkles, like a needle going through
stubborn material, and the flash of his chill
flesh as he rips past the bus queue
unbuttoning the heads behind, catches
up snags in the yarn of motives and bluff.

When girls shriek in the street at the threat
and predicament of this Jack-stripped-naked,
it is with no sense of whether he is risen
from a parched bed, or chases unbearable fact
from its prison of pretence. Those blame-smitten
faces that preen on salvation in starched wings
know no worse shame than to witness him act out
so woodenly a part written for supreme sweat.

Meantime, how does a nude man disappear?
Poor Adam, you can't go home again, not in that
condition. People are laughing; some pray
for police to come and gratify stranger urges.
Ought to be put away. What was he advertising?
But he ran round the corner, past the big display
where twenty different suits of the same cut
feign disbelief that he was ever here.

W. Price Turner

INTERVIEW

The weathercock has lost his golden skin
but now careers in more galvanic spin,
like a man with three telephones to attend,
furious and impatient to begin.

The steeplejack as he prepares to climb
knows that his labours are a waste of time.
Corruption in high places does not mend
by little brushes that flick off the grime

for paint to bless by ministry of height.
The creature looks surprised, and crows with might:
'Move with the wind or be replaced, my friend!'
He would spit in its eye, if wind were right.

Joy Udloff

IMAGE

I look into my mirror
And I see the face of a happy woman.
She is not happy because of this or that,
She is not glad, elated or even surprised.
She knows she is not a genius
Or a femme du monde
Or irresistible
Or such a success
And it has taken her twenty-five years
To learn all this
And her time has been foolishly spent
And her ways have been devious in the extreme.
This day for the first time
Her mirror reflects
Happiness, nothing less.

John Wain

COLLOQUIAL STANZAS TO A RADIO SET

Mad as an escaped herd, the dense air runs
Crowded and shouldering. Its voices crash
On the silence I sit in. Soft as drizzle
The dialects of the world soak into wall and carpet.

You offer your easy switch. *Care to voyage?*
Feel like a dip in meaning's river?
I hesitate, fingers stretched. Symphonies
Rain on the asbestos roof of my mind.

Chum, such global offers are no light matter.
Do I need the spray of oceans on my jacket?
My eyes water in the wind of disputation.
I get out of breath on the ladders of Babel.

Time was, to sit alone in a room was royal.
Books waited mutely like dogs for a muddy scamper:
Sometimes the tread of a friend was heard on the stair.
One's well-nourished identity crowded all spaces.

But my oblong friend has altered the nature of silence.
It is no longer simple like wood or oxygen.
Is stopping one's ears really a good habit?
Was that a nugget of truth just sailed past my ear?

Unlikely. At best what you offer is self-knowledge.
These drums of dissension echo my own ragged pulse.
Astronaut of the actual, I accept your challenge!
At the sharp core of the storm I already await you!

Vernon Watkins

FIDELITIES

The fountain gathers in a single jet
Fidelities where beams together run,
Thrives upon loss, enriches us with debt.

Nothing will match the day's full unison.
I love to see light break, and yet, and yet,
The final arbiter is not the sun.

Bounteous that brother, but he will forget
Others whose eyes the hand of death has closed,
Nor touch, nor seek them, when their light has set.

Seeing of what compound splendour life's composed,
Who could believe it now a part once played,
With so much owing to so many a ghost?

Of love's stern language noblest lives are made.
The shell of speech by many a voice is shot
Whose light, once kindled, cannot be betrayed.

A certain cadence underlies the plot;
However fatally the thread is spun,
The dying man can rise above his lot.

For me neglect and world-wide fame were one.
I was concerned with those the world forgot,
In the tale's ending saw its life begun;

And I was with them still when time was not.

Paddy Webb

JOURNEY TO THE SEA

Pale pool where two rills spill
By root of hemlock, hickory, and weeds of pickerel.
The lovely willow weeps and waves to her reflection,
Slim fingers slip to catch cool stones that flash,
Sparkle and splash as sunlight dapples in shadowy shallows
On weed-wearing patches of mud; where the
Queer pumping cry of the bird in the cattails is heard,
And, answering shrilly, in bubbles and trickles, are
Spring-peepers rippling the surface, wind-touched.
So slip to the edge and spill over, you eels,
Into the swift stream and straining water; splash
Through and under, twisting, turning, over and round
Where the ground in its flight falls, fresh river into the sea.

Dick Wilkinson

YOUNG BEECH

With one, sixty, perhaps three
Hundred years to go, here
Is one moment when the stem
Of a seedling after the good mast year
Indinges a touch of finger-thumb.
Annually enannuled can whose core
Die, coffined in heart wood,
But finger, living in leaves, leave
Only knuckle-bone, hard
Thing, jetsam of a soul that to grow alive
Had for sole interpreter, body.
Well, Athens had a body of slave
Labour to liberate the spirit: Working
In olive green or silver mine
Have grown such beeches as are breaking
Now into first leaf. A Parthenon.

Raymond Wilson

20TH CENTURY SONG

(Lullaby)

These supple vermin needle-eyed
Dance ring-a-roses all night long:
No floor-board shaking to your stride
Wholly obliterates their song.

The cellars of your ancestors
Are furred with filth that breathes and crawls;
Their bodies' sweat in slimed on floors,
And razor teeth attack the walls.

Obscenely copulating where
Your midnight feet unsurely walk,
No panelled wainscoting nor stair
Shuts out the horror of their talk.

Creep to your raftered attic's bed,
But do not dream yourself secure:
The ceiling cracks above your head
To distant plaudits from the sewer.

Soft-bodied, flopping from the rafter
With tooth, claw, stench, and corded tail,
Tomorrow night, or the night after,
They shall not fail. They shall not fail.

Hugo Williams

THE PICK-UP

The hardest part is conversation. That is
Always providing they both survive
The first shock of assault. The initial
Jolt. All doubt gone of a negative

Encounter, an enquiry as to the shortest
Route home. (A moment incidentally more
Unreal than sleep.) But know they tread
Tightropes like duellists and to gore

The enemy is to fall on one's sword.
Both guess at something more. The need
To escape. But the rules allow them
No more help. Now one must take the lead

And the hardest part begins. The same part
Played by the poet, all his senses alive
To the schemes in his head, the
Twicking of his thumbs, who yet cannot give

Through a certain reluctance to lie,
To commit himself. A virgin, his first
Words on the page will comprise
Their anxious overtures, carefully nursed

Into something like sanity by similar
Desires. Escape and the poem laid neat
In its place. Words having served their course,
The heart goes back to its simple beat.

David Wright

A VISION

I

In this mirror of paradise
Where we are not forsaken
Whose groves are green, and hours
Quartered with calamity,
Floats from the mountain's arm today's
Sun rising to redeem
Fantastic images,
Things being what they seem:
The valley of the beasts,
And plain of fruit and corn,
Immolations, miseries,
The rivers that rejoice,
And above them hovering birds.

II

Real vision where we move
In disgrace and in time
Disowners of the love,
Adherers to the crime,
Abstracted with that grief
With dingy tears to blind
And hearts not fit to break—
Tenants of heaven here and now:
Do you forgive your creatures
Who cannot hear the voice
With which all objects speak
The panic first command—
Simply to rejoice?

III

In the middle of the sky
At the dead pitch of noon
I see the golden ball:
Its clanging rays bear down
Echoing a serene
And terrifying light.
Over the fields and houses,
The failed hearts and false tongues,
The partial ecstasies and broken
Aspirations of delight,
I hear its bell-note call.
The eternity of a moment
In the gold sunstrokes held.

IV

Obedient to its law
Its zenith being found
That burning globe declines,
These shadows rake the ground.
The night climbs up the mountain's back
And with their foolish fires
Below the clouding dark
The cities prick the air.
The air is full of birds returning
And sun and beast go home,
The stars wheel over from the east
As the day reverts to the dead
Whose mysteries resume.

THE CONTRIBUTORS

DANNIE ABSE was born in Cardiff in 1923. He has published four books of poems including *Tenants Of The House* (1957) and *Poems, Golders Green* (1962); other publications include *Ash On A Young Man's Sleeve* (1954). He has had several plays produced, one of which, *House Of Cowards*, won the Charles Henry Foyle Award for 1960, and was included in J. C. Trewin's *Plays Of The Year: Number 23*. He is married, with three children, and lives in London. With Elizabeth Jennings and Stephen Spender he edited the fifth P.E.N. anthology, *New Poems—1956*. (Page 19.)

A. ALVAREZ was born in London in 1929, and educated at Corpus Christi College, Oxford. He has visited America several times, most recently as Visiting Professor of English at Brandeis University, Massachusetts. His publications include two books of criticism, *The Shaping Spirit* (1958) and *The School Of Donne* (1961), two pamphlets of poetry, and a Penguin anthology, *The New Poetry* (1962). He now lives in London and is a free-lance writer. (Pages 17 and 18.)

KINGSLEY AMIS was born in London in 1922, and educated at The City of London School and St John's, Oxford. He taught English for twelve years at the University College of Swansea, then became Fellow of English at Peterhouse, Cambridge. His publications include *A Frame Of Mind* (1953) and *A Case Of Samples* (1956) (verse); *Lucky Jim* (1954), *That Uncertain Feeling* (1955), *I Like It Here* (1958), and *Take A Girl Like You* (1960) (novels); *New Maps Of Hell* (1960) (belles-lettres); and *My Enemy's Enemy* (short stories). He is married, with three children, and now lives abroad. (Page 15.)

ALASDAIR ASTON was born in 1930 and educated at Framlingham College, Suffolk, and Pembroke College, Cambridge, where he was awarded the Chancellor's Medal in 1953. He is Senior English Master at Alleyn's School, Dulwich. This is the first poem he has published since leaving Cambridge. (Page 16.)

ANDREW BAILY was born at West Malling, Kent, in 1937, and educated at Blundell's School, Tiverton, Devon. He was brought up in Glastonbury, Somerset, and now shares a flat in Cambridge with his twin brother Edward, who also writes poems. Andrew Baily's first published poems appeared in *New Poems—1962*. (Page 20.)

JACK BEECHING served in the Royal Navy during the war; for most of the time since he has lived by his writing. He has published historical and critical work as well as novels, but his vocation is poetry and his books of poems include *Aspects Of Love, Truth Is A Naked Lady*, and (forthcoming) *Never But Now*. He is married to Alexis Brown, who writes stories for children, and they live in Spain. (Page 21.)

CARL BODE was born in 1911 and educated at the University of Chicago and Northwestern University. He is Professor of English at the University of Maryland but was on leave from 1957 to 1959 as cultural attaché to the American Embassy in London. His most recent works include *The Man Behind You* (poems) (1959, U.K.; 1960, U.S.A.); *The Anatomy Of American Popular Culture 1840–1861* (cultural history) (1959: U.S.A.) and *The Great Experiment In American Literature* (1961: U.K. and U.S.A.), a volume of literary criticism, Mr. Bode being editor and contributor. He is married, and lives in Maryland, U.S.A. (Page 23.)

BARRY BOWES was born in Shepperton in 1940, but lived in Wallasey from 1945 until 1962 when he moved to London. He was educated at Oldershaw Grammar School. He now works as an assistant librarian. (Page 22.)

PAUL CASIMIR was born in Jersey in 1922 of Polish and Channel Island parents. He was educated at Victoria College, Jersey, and came to England after the war and was a college librarian in Hertfordshire where he lived with his wife, twin sons, and a daughter. He published two booklets of verse and his poems were published in various anthologies, periodicals, and on the B.B.C. At the time of his tragically early death in November 1962, following an operation, he was working on an anthology of poems by inmates of Nazi Concentration Camps; his widow is continuing work on this volume which was to have been called *A Tree From The Dust.* No publication date can yet be given. (Page 26.)

CHARLES CAUSLEY was born in 1917 at Launceston, Cornwall, where he still writes and teaches. He is a Fellow of the Royal Society of Literature. His publications include *Farewell Aggie Weston, Survivor's Leave, Union Street, Johnny Alleluia* (poems); *Hands To Dance* (short stories), and *Dawn and Dusk,* an anthology of modern verse for children. He edited *Peninsula,* an anthology of West Country verse. (Page 24).

RICHARD CHURCH was born in London in 1893, and published his first book of verse in 1917. At first a Civil Servant and colleague of Humbert Wolfe, he has for the last thirty-three years been a free-lance writer and literary adviser. He has published some fifty books, including his *Collected Poems,* published in 1948, and his most recent book *Prince Albert* (1963). He was awarded *The Sunday Times*' Prize for Literature in 1955 for his autobiography *Over The Bridge,* and was made a C.B.E. in 1957. He has also been awarded the Femina Vie Heureuse and Foyle Poetry Prizes, and from 1957 to 1959 was President of the English Centre of P.E.N. He is married, and lives in Kent. (Pages 27 and 28.)

ROBERT CONQUEST was born in Great Malvern, Worcestershire, in 1917, and was educated at Winchester and Magdalen College, Oxford. He edited the two *New Lines* (anthologies), writes criticism for *The Spectator* and *The Guardian,* and his publications include *Poems* and *Between Mars and Venus.* With Michael Hamburger and Howard Sergeant he edited the second P.E.N. anthology, *New Poems—1953.* He has two sons, and lives in London (Page 30.)

HILARY CORKE was born in 1921 at Malvern, Worcestershire, and educated at Charterhouse and Christ Church, Oxford. He was formerly Lecturer in Medieval English at the Universities of Cairo and Edinburgh, and is now a free-lance writer. He has published one collection of verse, *The Early Drowned,* and a long poem, *Adam Awake* (*1961*). With William Plomer and Anthony Thwaite, he edited the ninth P.E.N.

anthology, *New Poems—1961*. He is married and lives with his wife and three children in Abinger Hammer, Surrey. (Page 32.)

MARTIN DANIEL was born in 1932, and educated at Leeds Grammar School and Oxford and Manchester Universities. Although he has been writing poetry since childhood, he recently burnt almost all of it and started again. He is at present engaged on a study of the French poet Supervielle. He is married, has three children, and lives in Norwich, Norfolk. (Page 36.)

DONALD DAVIE was born in 1922 in Barnsley, Yorkshire, and educated at Barnsley Grammar School and St Catharine's College, Cambridge. He then became a Fellow of Trinity College, Dublin, and Lecturer in English in Dublin University. He is now a Fellow of Gonville and Caius College, Cambridge, and University Lecturer in English. His publications include *Purity Of Diction In English Verse*, *Brides Of Reason* (poems); and *The Forests Of Lithuania* (1960, an adaptation from Polish, Marvell Press); and a work spoken on a gramophone record, *A Sequence For Francis Parkman* (1960, Marvell Press). He is married, with three children, and lives in Cambridge. (Page 35.)

C. DAY LEWIS was born in 1904 of Anglo-Irish parentage, and educated at Sherborne School and Wadham College, Oxford. He was made a C.B.E. in 1950, and from 1951 to 1956 was Professor of Poetry in the University of Oxford. He is a Vice-President of the Royal Society of Literature. His publications include *Pegasus And Other Poems*, *The Poetic Image*, *Collected Poems—1954*, *The Buried Day* (1960, autobiography); *The Gate* (poems), and other books of verse and criticism, as well as his children's books such as *The Otterbury Incident*, also detective stories under the pseudonym of Nicholas Blake. He has four children, is married to Jill Balcon, and lives in Greenwich. With Kathleen Nott and Thomas Blackburn, he edited the sixth P.E.N. anthology, *New Poems—1957*. (Page 37.)

CLIFFORD DYMENT was born in the Midlands in 1914, of Welsh parentage. He was educated at elementary schools and Loughborough Grammar School, and has worked as shop-assistant, travelling salesman, clerk, book-reviewer, documentary and television film director. He is now a freelance writer and broadcaster. He has received an Atlantic Award, and been elected a Fellow of the Royal Society of Literature. His books of poems include *Poems 1935-1948* and *Experiences And Places.* He recently published an early autobiography, *The Railway Game.* He is married and lives in London. With Roy Fuller and the late Montagu Slater he edited the first P.E.N. anthology, *New Poems—1952.* (Page 38.)

JULIAN ENNIS was born in 1915, and read English at Merton College, Oxford, 1934–7, being tutored by Edmund Blunden. He took the Diploma Course at Oxford Department of Education from 1937 to 1938, and has been a schoolmaster since 1939. He has written and edited many school textbooks. He lives in Windsor, Berkshire. (Page 41.)

D. J. ENRIGHT was born in 1920, and has taught English literature in Alexandria, Birmingham, Japan, Berlin, and Bangkok. He is at present Professor of English at the University of Singapore. His publications include three novels, a book on Japan (*The World Of Dew*), a collection of critical essays, and four volumes of poetry of which the most recent are *Some Men Are Brothers* and *Addictions* (Chatto and Windus, 1962). (Pages 39 and 40).

NISSIM EZEKIEL was born in 1924 in Bombay, India, and educated there. He is Professor of English Literature and Head of the English Department in the M.M. College of Arts, Vilé Parlé (West), affiliated to the University of Bombay. He is the former editor, and present Book Reviews Editor, of *Quest,* a quarterly of politics, philosophy and literature, also the associate-editor of *Imprint,* a books monthly. He has published four collections of verse, *A Time To Change* (Fortune Press, London, 1952), *Sixty Poems* (1953), and *The Third* (1958) published in Bombay, and *The Unfinished Man* (1959) published by The Writers' Workshop, Calcutta. (Page 42.)

JOHN FAIRFAX was born in 1931, and has had his poems published in English, American, French, and German magazines. No book but MS. in throes. He lives in an ivory conning-tower of flint and straw between Hermitage and Yattenden, Berkshire. (Page 43.)

JOAN FORMAN was born in 1919 in Louth, Lincolnshire, and has lived since in various parts of England. She was educated at Alfred Lord Tennyson's old school, the King Edward VI Grammar School in Louth. She wrote the poetry page feature in *John O' London's*, and short stories, poetry, criticism, and general articles for many magazines. She has eight short plays in publication (with Evans Brothers, H. F. W. Deane and Son, and The Epworth Press); two of her plays have so far been professionally performed and a third was the runner-up in a Bridie Memorial Competition. She has just completed her first novel, *Towards The Tower* which will appear in 1964. She lives in Lincolnshire. (Pages 44 and 45.)

EDGAR FOXALL was born in 1906 in Whitby, Wirral, Cheshire, and educated at council schools. He worked in the steel industry at fourteen, and throughout the 'slump' period of the thirties. When the works closed in 1944, after a period on the 'dole' he became a schoolteacher in secondary modern and primary schools. He contributed to a number of periodicals during the thirties, and has published three books of verse, *Water Rat Sonata* (1940), *Poems* (1947), and *Decade* (1957). (Page 46.)

G. S. FRASER was born in Glasgow in 1915, and educated at Aberdeen Grammar School and St Andrew's University, Scotland. His books include *Vision And Rhetoric*, *News From South America*, *The Modern Writer And His World*, etcetera. Since 1958 he has been Lecturer in English Literature at Leicester University, and is at present visiting Professor at Rochester University, N. Y. He is married and has three children. (Pages 48 and 49.)

ROY FULLER was born in Failsworth, Manchester, in 1912. He is the solicitor to a large London Building Society and legal adviser to The Building Societies' Association. He has one son, who is also a poet. He has published seven books of verse, one of which, *Brutus's Orchard*, received an Arts Council Prize in 1959; his *Collected Poems* appeared in 1962. He has written criticism for *The London Magazine*, *The Listener*, etcetera. He is also a novelist—*The Ruined Boys*, *The Father's Comedy* (1961) and many others; his latest, *The Perfect Fool*, appeared in the summer of 1963. With Clifford Dyment and the late Montagu Slater he edited the first P.E.N. anthology, *New Poems—1952*. (Page 50.)

KAREN GERSHON is Jewish, and was born in Germany in 1923, and came to England in 1938. Her first novel was published in 1956, and her first collection of poems was included in *New Poets 1959*; her second collection, *A Sense Of The Past*, is awaiting publication. Since 1950 she has lived in Somerset, and is married with four children. (Page 53.)

ZULFIKAR GHOSE was born in Sialkot, Pakistan, in 1935, and educated at schools in Bombay and Chelsea, and at Keele University. At present he is living in London where he works as a cricket and hockey correspondent of *The Observer*, reviews books for *The Western Daily Press* (Bristol), and broadcasts. His poems have been published in England, India, and the United States. He has written one prose work, an autobiography, *Confessions Of A Native-Alien*. (Page 54.)

GORDON GRIDLEY was born in 1931 and educated at Tottenham Grammar School and Trent Park Training College, Hertfordshire. He now lives and teaches in Essex. (Pages 55 and 56.)

THOM GUNN was born in 1929 in Gravesend, Kent, and educated at Trinity College, Cambridge, at St John's College, Cambridge, and Stanford University, California. He received the Somerset Maugham Award in 1959 and used it to live in Berlin in 1960. His books published include *Fighting Terms* (1954), *The Sense Of Movement* (1957), *My Sad Captains* (1961), and *Selected Poems* (with Ted Hughes, 1962). He now lives in San Francisco. (Pages 57 and 58.)

MARY HACKER was born in London in 1908, and educated at Trowbridge High School and Southampton University

College, reading Early and Modern French. Her poems and short stories have been published in various periodicals, and she has written two novels, *The Charming Boy* and *The Kind Young Man*. She is married, has a daughter and two sons, and lives in Harpenden, Hertfordshire. (Page 61.)

MICHAEL HAMBURGER was born in 1924 and educated at Westminster School and Christ Church, Oxford. He has published four books of poems, the last two being *The Dual Site* and *Weather and Season* (1963 Longmans). He has also published critical essays and translations, of which the most recent are *Modern German Poetry 1910–1960* (co-edited with Christopher Middleton) and *Hofmannsthal: Plays And Libretti*. He is married and lives in Berkshire. With Robert Conquest and Howard Sergeant, he edited the second P.E.N. anthology, *New Poems—1953*. (Page 64.)

GEORGE ROSTREVOR HAMILTON was born in 1888, and educated at Bradfield and Exeter College, Oxford, where he took a first-class degree in Honour Mods. and in Greats. He was Presiding Special Commissioner of Income Tax from 1950 to 1953, and was knighted in 1951. His many books include *Collected Poems And Epigrams* (1958) also criticism and philosophy. He is married and lives in Blackheath. (Pages 59 and 60.)

NORMAN HARVEY was born in Bristol in 1921, and teaches mathematics in Guildford, Surrey. His poems have appeared in various magazines, newspapers, and anthologies. With a co-editor, he edited an *Anthology Of Bristol Poetry* and later edited *Unicorn*, the poetry quarterly published by the South-Western Arts Association. (Page 63.)

JOHN HEATH-STUBBS was born in London in 1918. He read English at Queen's College, Oxford, and has since worked as a private tutor, schoolmaster and publisher's hack. He was Visiting Professor of English at Alexandria University, and held the same post at the University of Michigan from 1960 to 1961. His publications include *Wounded Thamuz, Beauty And The Beast, The Divided Ways, The Swarming Of The Bees, A Charm Against The*

Toothache, The Triumph Of The Muse, Helen In Egypt, and *The Blue-Fly In His Head* (O.U.P. 1962). He lives in London. (Page 118.)

JOHN HORDER was born in Brighton in 1936, and from St Paul's School went to Selwyn College, Cambridge, when he published poems and reviews in *The Cambridge Review, Delta, Granta,* and also did a series of interviews of young writers for the B.B.C. In 1961 he gave an impromptu reading of his poetry on the first evening of the Mermaid Festival of Poetry in London's Mermaid Theatre, and has recently published poems in *John O' London's, Tribune,* and *Envoi.* At present he works as Literary Adviser to Constable's, writes occasional pieces for *The Guardian* and interviews regularly for the B.B.C. (Page 65.)

TED HUGHES was born at Mytholmroyd, West Yorkshire, in 1930, and from Mexborough Grammar School went to Pembroke College, Cambridge. His publications include *The Hawk In The Rain* (1957) and *Lupercal* (1960). He was married to the late Sylvia Plath and lives in Devonshire with his two small children. With Patricia Beer and Vernon Scannell, he edited the tenth P.E.N. anthology, *New Poems—1962.* (Pages 66 and 67.)

ZOFIA ILINSKA is Polish, and was born in 1921. She went to school in Poland, then to Reading University where she read English. Her publications in Polish include a book of poems *Duch Lorda Curzona* and a translation of T. S. Eliot's *Murder In The Cathedral.* She can no longer write in Polish, and has 'gone over' entirely into English. Her English poems have appeared in several P.E.N. anthologies, in Guinness Books of Poetry, and other anthologies and magazines. She wrote a play for the B.B.C. Third Programme, *Night In Lamorran*, has a book of poems ready for publication, and is working on another play and another book of poems. She now lives in Cornwall. (Page 68.)

ELIZABETH JENNINGS was born in Lincolnshire in 1926 and educated at Oxford High School and St. Anne's College, Oxford. From 1950 to 1958 she was Assistant Librarian in Oxford City Library, later working for Chatto and Windus as an editorial assistant, but now devotes her time to her own writing. She is working on her fifth book of poems; her first won an Arts Council Prize, her second the Somerset Maugham Award for 1956. She has also published a book about poetry for children, a pamphlet on contemporary poetry for the British Council, a translation of Michelangelo's Sonnets, collaborated on a translation of a play by Calderon, edited an anthology, and wrote a study of the relations between mystical experience and the making of poems entitled *Every Changing Shape*. She lives in Oxford. With Dannie Abse and Stephen Spender, she edited the fifth P.E.N. anthology, *New Poems—1956*. (Page 70.)

RICHARD KELL was born in County Cork, South Ireland, in 1927, and educated in South India, Belfast, and Dublin, graduating from Trinity College, Dublin. In addition to his poems (many of which have been broadcast and published) he has written short stories and essays, and has also written a novella. His first collection of poems was *Control Tower* (1962) and his work was included in *Six Irish Poets* (1962). He is at present teaching in a London technical college, is married with four children, and lives in Twickenham. (Page 73.)

JAMES KIRKUP was born in 1918, and educated at South Shields High School and Durham University. He won the Atlantic Award in Literature (Rockefeller Foundation) in 1950, and was first holder of the Gregory Fellowship in Poetry at Leeds University. He was Visiting Poet at the Bath Academy of Art 1953–6; Lecturer in English for the Swedish Ministry of Education in Stockholm 1956–7; Professor of English at Salamanca University 1957–8, at Tohoku University, Sendai, Japan 1958–61, and was briefly at the University of Malaya, Kuala Lumpur, in 1962. He has published eight books of poetry, the latest being *Refusal To Conform*; two volumes of autobiography, *The Only Child* and *Sorrows, Passions and Alarms*; a large number of translations, plays, radio and TV scripts, including *The True Mistery Of The Nativity* and *The True Mistery Of The Passion*; also two travel books *These Horned Islands: A Journal Of Japan*, and *Tropic Temper: A Memoir of Malaya*, and a novel, *The*

Love Of Others. He is a contributor to the B.B.C., *The Listener, The Spectator, The Times Literary Supplement, Time And Tide, Botteghe Oscure, The New Yorker*, etcetera. He was recently elected a Fellow of the Royal Society of Literature. He is now living in Tokyo, where he is Literary Editor of *Orient-West Magazine*. (Pages 74 and 76.)

OONAGH LAHR was born in London in 1929 and educated by her father, Charles Lahr, and St Martin's Convent School, at the Woodhouse School in North London, the University of London, the University of Bristol, and the Shakespeare Institute of the University of Birmingham. She is a fugitive from the teaching profession, since she would not now willingly support the English educational system, and an alumna of Holloway Prison for her Committee of 100 activities (where she wrote her potted biography, when becoming a civil instead of an ordinary prisoner: On Hard Lines:

One who on hard beds
Dreamt long and deep
Moved to a softer bed
Now cannot sleep).

She suddenly started to write poetry when twenty-eight, as an alternative to a nervous breakdown. She lives with her parents in Muswell Hill, London. (Page 79.)

PHILIP LARKIN was born in 1922, and educated at King Henry VII School, Coventry, and St John's College, Oxford. He has published a novel, *A Girl In Winter*, and two collections of poems, *The North Ship* and *The Less Deceived*. He is Librarian to the University of Hull and, with Bonamy Dobrée and the late Louis MacNeice, edited the seventh P.E.N. anthology, *New Poems—1958*, which was the Christmas Choice of The Poetry Book Society. (Page 81.)

B. C. LEALE was born in Ashford, Middlesex, in 1930, and educated at the Municipal College, Southend. He has contributed poems to *The Listener, The Observer*, and *The Times Literary Supplement*, and has a volume of poems in preparation. He is now employed as a bookseller's assistant, and lives in London. (Pages 77 and 78.)

JOHN LEHMANN was born in 1907 and educated at Eton (King's Scholar) and Trinity College, Cambridge. He published his first book of poems, *A Garden Revisited*, in 1931. His *Collected Poems* (1963) contains all the poems he wishes to keep. He both founded and edited *New Writing* in 1936, and *The London Magazine* in 1954. He has written criticism and a novel; two volumes of autobiography *The Whispering Gallery* (1955), *I Am My Brother* (1960); also *Ancestors And Friends* (1962). He edited *The Chatto Book Of Modern Poetry* (with C. Day Lewis, 1956) and *The Craft Of Letters In England* (a Symposium published on the occasion of the London Congress of International P.E.N., Cresset Press, 1956). He was a publisher for many years, and now lives in London. (Page 82.)

EDWARD LUCIE-SMITH was born in 1933 in Kingston, Jamaica, British West Indies, and educated at King's School, Canterbury, and Merton College, Oxford. He works as a copy-writer in an advertising agency, writes art-criticism and book-reviews, broadcasts, and teaches at a London County Council Evening College. He has published one book of poems, *A Tropical Childhood*, which was joint-winner of the John Llewellyn Rhys Award for 1962, and is co-editor of a new anthology, *A Group Anthology*. He lives in Chelsea, London. (Page 108.)

GEORGE MACBETH was born at Shotts, Lanarkshire, in 1932, and educated at King Edward VII School, Sheffield, and New College, Oxford. He has published three books of poems, *A Form Of Words*, *Lecture To The Trainees* and *The Broken Places*, and is editing *The Penguin Book Of Sick Verse*. He now works for the B.B.C. as editor and producer of *New Comment*, *The Poet's Voice*, and other programmes. He is married, and lives in Richmond, Surrey. (Pages 83 and 85.)

R. S. MORGAN was born in 1938. (Page 86.)

NUMA CLIVE NEGRI was born in 1934. His formal education was predominantly scientific and between 1954 and 1955 he served as climatologist on an expedition to the Arctic. During recent years he has developed a profound interest in philosophy and the social sciences. His publications include *The Valley Of Shadows* (travel) and *Art Contra Science* (sociology). He is at present engaged upon a philosophical treatise entitled *Criteria Aesthetica*. He lives in Twickenham, Middlesex. (Page 87.)

HUBERT NICHOLSON was born in Hull in 1908. He is a sub-editor at Reuters and lives in Fleet Street. His published works include *Half My Days And Nights* and *A Voyage To Wonderland* (essays); *The Mirage In The South* (poems); *Little Heyday, Sunk Island, Mr. Hill And Friends*, etcetera. He is at present working on a play. (Page 88.)

KATHLEEN NOTT was born in London in 1910, and educated at Oxford. She is a lecturer, reviewer, and broadcaster on philosophical subjects and is Chairman of the P.E.N. Poetry Committee. She has published three novels, *Mile End, The Dry Deluge*, and *Private Fires*; three volumes of verse, *Landscapes And Departures, Poems From The North*, and *Creatures And Emblems*; also *The Emperor's Clothes* (criticism) and *A Clean, Well-Lighted Place* (a book on Sweden). She lives in London. With Thomas Blackburn and C. Day Lewis, she edited the sixth P.E.N. anthology, *New Poems—1957*. (Page 89.)

MERVYN PEAKE was born in Tientsin, China, in 1911, and educated at Tientsin Grammar School, and Eltham College, Kent, later in the Academy Schools. His illustrated books include *The Ancient Mariner, Treasure Island, The Hunting Of The Snark*, etcetera. He has published a trilogy, *Titus Groan, Gormenghast* (which won, with his poem *The Glassblowers*, the W. H. Heinemann Foundation Award for Literature) and *Titus Alone*. His books of poems include *Shapes And Sounds* and *The Rhyme Of The Flying Bomb*. His play, *The Wit To Woo*, was produced at the Arts Theatre, London, the Playhouse, Oxford, and The Arts, Cambridge. He is also the author and illustrator of many children's books, *Captain Slaughterboard Drops Anchor, Letters From A Lost Uncle, Rhymes Without Reason*, etcetera. He is also a painter and has held many exhibitions in London, New York, and Dublin. His wife Maeve Gilmore is also an artist, and they live in London with their one daughter and two sons. (Page 92.)

SYLVIA PLATH was born in Boston, Massachusetts, in 1932, and she was a graduate of Smith College and Cambridge University, winning a Fulbright Grant for 1955–7. Her poems appeared in many periodicals, and a volume of them, *The Colossus*, was published in England by Heinemann and in America by Alfred Knopf. She was married to Ted Hughes. She died in 1963, leaving a small son and daughter. (Pages 93 and 94.)

PETER REDGROVE was born in 1932 and educated at Taunton School and Queens' College, Cambridge—to which he won Open and State Scholarships in Natural Sciences. Until recently he was in America on a Fulbright Scholarship, where he taught as 'visiting poet' at the University of Buffalo, New York. He is now Gregory Fellow in Poetry at Leeds University. He has published two books of poetry, *The Collector And Other Poems* (1960) and *The Nature Of Cold Weather And Other Poems* (1961) which was a Poetry Book Society Choice. A new collection, *At The White Monument*, is due out in the autumn, 1963. He is married and living in Leeds. (Pages 96 and 97.)

CHRISTOPHER SCAIFE was born in 1900 and educated at St George's, Harpenden, King's College, London, and St John's College, Oxford. He won the Newdigate Prize for English Verse in 1923, was a contributor to *King's Verse* in 1918, and to *Oxford Verse 1922–1923*. His verse play, *Death's Triumph*, was performed at the Barn Theatre, Oxted, in 1924 and at the Oxford Playhouse in 1926; *A Christmas Play*, written for St Mary's Church, Oxford, was performed there in 1933. His published volumes of poetry include *Towards Corinth, O Englishman* (1934), *A Latter-Day Athenian* (1937), *In Middle Age* (1953), *Morning, Noon And Night* (1955), *In The Levant* (1958). The title poem of *A Latter Day Athenian* was set to music by John Gardner, commissioned by the Oxford University Press, and was performed by The Elizabethan Singers at the Wigmore Hall in June 1962. He is now Professor of English at the American University of Beirut in the Lebanon. (Page 98.)

VERNON SCANNELL was born in 1922, and was once a prize-fighter. He has made a number of broadcasts for the B.B.C. and now works as a free-lance writer. He has contributed to various periodicals, and his publications include *Graves And Resurrections*, *A Mortal Pitch*, *The Masks Of Love*, and *A Sense Of Danger* (poems); *The Fight* and *The Face Of The Enemy* (novels); and *The Shadowed Place* (thriller). He is married, with four children, and lives in Limpsfield, Surrey. With Patricia Beer and Ted Hughes, he edited the tenth P.E.N. anthology, *New Poems—1962*. (Page 100.)

JON SILKIN was born in 1930 in London, and educated at Wycliffe College and Dulwich. He was Gregory Fellow in Poetry at Leeds University from 1958 to 1960. His publications include *The Peaceable Kingdom*, *The Two Freedoms*, and *The Re-Ordering Of The Stones*. He edited an anthology of contemporary verse, *Living Voices* for Vista Books, and is the editor of the literary magazine, *Stand*. He is married, and lives in Leeds. With Anthony Cronin and Terence Tiller he edited the eighth P.E.N. anthology, *New Poems—1960*. (Page 107.)

EDITH SITWELL, sister of Sir Osbert Sitwell and Sacheverell Sitwell, was born in Scarborough and educated privately. She was created a D.B.E. in 1954, and is an Honorary Doctor of Literature of Oxford, Durham, Leeds, and Sheffield Universities. Her publications include *Clowns' Houses*, *Bucolic Comedies*, *Sleeping Beauty*, *Elegy On Dead Fashion*, *Gold Coast Customs*, *Alexander Pope*, *Collected Poems—1930* (also in 1954, New York, and 1957, England), *Aspects Of Modern Poetry*, *Victoria Of England*, *Trio*, *Street Songs*, *A Poet's Notebook*, *A Song Of The Cold*, *Fanfare For Elizabeth* and *The Queens And The Hive*, *A Notebook On William Shakespeare*, *The Canticle Of The Rose*, *Gardeners And Astronomers*, *The English Eccentrics*, *Green Song*, and *The Outcasts* (Macmillan, 1962); she edited *The Pleasures Of Poetry* and *The Atlantic Book Of English And American Poetry* (1958, U.S.A., 1959, U.K.). She now lives in Hampstead, London. (Pages 101 and 103.)

STEVIE SMITH was born in Hull and educated at Palmer's Green High School and North London Collegiate School for Girls. She has worked in a publisher's office, and has written criticism for *The Observer*, *The Spectator*, *The Daily Telegraph*, *Time And*

Tide, The Listener, The Times Literary Supplement, etcetera. Her publications include *Novel On Yellow Paper, Over The Frontier*, and *The Holiday* (novels); *A Good Time Was Had By All, Tender Only To One, Mother, What Is Man?, Harold's Leap* (poems); *Not Waving But Drowning* (poems and drawings); also *Cats In Colour* and *Some Are More Human Than Others* (sketch book). Her *Selected Poems* appeared in 1962. She lives in Palmer's Green, London. (Pages 111 and 114.)

BERNARD SPENCER was born in 1909 and educated at Marlborough and Corpus Christi, Oxford. He worked for the British Council in Greece, Egypt, Spain, Italy, Turkey, and in Vienna until his accidental death in 1963. His publications include *Aegean Islands* and *The Twist In The Plotting* (1960, limited edition by Reading University School of Fine Arts) and *With Luck Lasting* (Hodder and Stoughton, June 1963). (Page 115.)

STEPHEN SPENDER was born in 1909, and educated at University College School and University College, Oxford. He was co-editor of *Horizon* magazine from 1939 to 1941, was a fireman in the National Fire Service from 1941 to 1944, Counsellor, Section of Letters, UNESCO, 1947, and since 1953 has been co-editor of *Encounter*. He was made a C.B.E. in 1962. His publications include *The Still Centre, Trial Of A Judge, Ruins And Visions, The Destructive Element, The Creative Element, The Making Of A Poem, Engaged In Writing* (stories); *Learning Laughter* (travels in Israel); *World Within World* (autobiography) and a translation of Schiller's *Mary Stuart*. He is married, with a son and daughter, and lives in London. With Dannie Abse and Elizabeth Jennings, he edited the fifth P.E.N. anthology, *New Poems—1956*. (Page 105.)

DEREK STANFORD was born in Middlesex in 1918, and educated at Upper Latymer School, London, and studied for the Law. He is a lecturer and literary journalist. His publications include *Music For Statues* and, with John Bayliss, *A Romantic Miscellany* (poems); *John Betjeman: A Study*; *Muriel Spark: A Medallion*; *The Body Of Love* (anthology); *Christopher Fry: An Appreciation*; *The Freedom Of Poetry*. Also, in collaboration with Muriel Spark, *Tribute to Wordsworth, My Best Mary* (letters to Mary Shelley), and

Emily Brontë: Her Life And Work. He lives in Westcliff-on-Sea, Essex. (Page 117)

R. S. THOMAS was born in 1913. His publications include *Song At The Year's Turning* (1955) and *Poetry For Supper* (1958). He lives in Wales. (Page 123.)

ANTHONY THWAITE was born in Chester in 1930, and educated at Kingswood School and Christ Church, Oxford. He has been a lecturer in Japan, worked as a B.B.C. producer for four years, and is at present the literary editor of *The Listener.* He has published two books of poems, *Home Truths* (1957), *The Owl In The Tree* (1963), and *Contemporary English Poetry: An Introduction* (1959). He is married, has three daughters, and lives in Richmond, Surrey. With Hilary Corke and William Plomer, he edited the ninth P.E.N. anthology, *New Poems—1961.* (Pages 120 and 121.)

TERENCE TILLER was born in Cornwall in 1916. He was awarded the Chancellor's Gold Medal for English Verse at Cambridge in 1936. Since 1946 he has worked in the B.B.C. Features Department as writer-producer. With Jon Silkin and Anthony Cronin, he edited the eighth P.E.N. anthology, *New Poems—1960.* (Pages 124 and 125.)

CHARLES TOMLINSON was born in 1927, and educated at Queen's College, Cambridge, and the University of London. He lectures at Bristol University and is currently at the University of New Mexico. His work first won widespread acclaim in the U.S.A. where he has won several poetry prizes, besides a travelling fellowship from the Institute of International Education. His published work includes *The Necklace* (1955), *Seeing Is Believing*, and *Versions From Fyodor Tyutchev* (1960). His most recent book of poems, *A People Landscape*, appeared in 1962. He recently completed *Castilian Ilexes*, a book of verse translations from Antonio Machado. (Page 126.)

W. PRICE TURNER was born in York in 1927. He was Gregory Fellow in Poetry at the University of Leeds from 1960 to 1962, and is now free-lancing again as a writer and lecturer. His collections of poetry are *First Offence*, *The Rudiment Of An Eye*, and *The Flying Corset*. He now lives in Leeds. (Pages 127 and 128.)

JOY UDLOFF was born in 1934, and educated at King Edward's High School, Birmingham, and Leeds University. She was an Administrative Officer of the London Council for three years, and is now teaching English in New Zealand. Her poems have appeared in *Outposts*, *Universities Poetry I*, *Phoenix*, and *Poetry And Audience*, but it has been her life-long ambition to have a poem appearing in a P.E.N. anthology. (Page 129.)

JOHN WAIN was born in Stoke-on-Trent, Staffordshire, in 1925, and educated at the High School, Newcastle-under-Lyme, and St John's College, Oxford. He was Fereday Fellow at St John's College, Oxford, from 1946 to 1949, and Lecturer in English Literature at the University of Reading from 1947 to 1955, when he resigned to become a free-lance author and critic. His career since has involved editing, lecturing in three continents, film and dramatic criticism, radio and television work, etcetera. He was Director of the Poetry Book Society's 'Poetry At The Mermaid Festival', London, 1961. His publications include *Hurry On Down*, *Living In The Present*, *The Contenders*, *A Travelling Woman*, *Strike The Father Dead* (novels); *Nuncle* (short stories); *Preliminary Essays* (criticism); *A Word Carved On A Sill* and *Weep Before God* (poetry). He is married, and has two sons. (Page 130.)

VERNON WATKINS was born in Wales in 1906, and educated at Repton and Magdalene College, Cambridge. He entered Lloyds Bank in 1925 and is still an official therein. He served in the R.A.F. from 1941 to 1946. His first book, *Ballad Of The Mari Lwyd And Other Poems*, was reissued in 1960, and other publications include *The Lamp And The Veil*, *The Lady With The Unicorn*, *The Death Bell*, *Poems And Ballads*, *Selected Poems*, and *The North Sea* (translation of Heine's poems), also *Cypress And Acacia* and *Affinities* (1962). He edited *Letters To Vernon Watkins By Dylan Thomas*. Since 1912 he has lived near Swansea, and is married with a daughter and four sons. (Page 131.)

PADDY WEBB was born in 1923, and educated at St Angela's Convent, Forest Gate, London. During the war she worked at the Bank of England and as a V.A.D. She was married in 1943 and has three children, and divorced in 1960. From 1959 to 1962 she trained for teaching at Portsmouth and Bognor colleges. Although she has written a large number of poems over a period of some years, she has never before attempted to have them published. She now lives in Bognor Regis, Sussex, with her children, and teaches English and Art at the Modern School there. (Page 132.)

DICK WILKINSON was born in 1926, educated at Preston Grammar School, served with the army in India and then read Classics at Cambridge. His first book, *Slates Of Opal* (Mitre Press), is a selection of poems written in his twenties, some of them in the Fell country of north-west England where he is a forestry worker. (Page 133.)

HUGO WILLIAMS was born in Windsor in 1942, and educated at Eton. He then worked on *The London Magazine* for two years, and had about twenty-five poems published in various places. At present he has a book of verse at a publisher's and is working on a novel. He lives in London, but is now in Kashmir on his way round the world. (Page 135.)

RAYMOND WILSON was born in 1925, and educated at University College, London. He has edited a *Selection Of Coleridge*, and has co-edited several school anthologies. His poems have appeared in various periodicals and have been broadcast. He is now Senior English Master at Dulwich College, London. (Page 134.)

DAVID WRIGHT was born in Johannesburg in 1920, and educated at Northampton School For The Deaf and Oriel College, Oxford. His publications include *Poems*, *Moral Stories*, *Monologue Of A Deaf Man* and a prose translation of *Beowulf*. He edits *X*, the quarterly magazine of literature and art, and edited *The Faber Book Of Twentieth-Century Verse*. He is married, and lives in London. (Page 136.)

THE EDITOR

LAWRENCE DURRELL was born in India in 1912, and educated at St Joseph's College, Darjeeling, India, and St Edmund's School, Canterbury. He became a Fellow of the Royal Society of Literature in 1954. He has been Senior Press Officer to the British Embassies in Athens and Cairo, and Press Attaché in Alexandria and Belgrade, Director of the British Institutes in Kalamata, Greece, and Cordoba, Argentina, and Director of Public Relations in the Dodecanese Islands and later to the Government of Cyprus. His publications include *Panic Spring*, *The Black Book*, *Cefalu*, *Prospero's Cell*, *Reflections On A Marine Venus*, *Bitter Lemons* (which won the Duff Cooper Memorial Award for 1957), and *The Alexandria Quartet* (novels); *White Eagles Over Serbia* (for children); *A Key To Modern Poetry* (criticism); *Esprit de Corps* and *Stiff Upper Lip* (humour); *Pope Joan* and *Four Greek Poets* (translations); *Sappho* and *An Irish Faustus* (plays); also *Private Country*, *Cities, Plains And People*, *On Seeming To Presume*, *Tree Of Idleness*, *Selected Poems* (poetry). His *Collected Poems* were published in 1960. He married for the third time in 1961, has two daughters, and lives in France.